THE SPIRIT OF THE GAME

THE SPIRIT OF THE GAME

EXCEPTIONAL PHOTOGRAPHS FROM THE HOCKEY HALL OF FAME

TRIUMPH

EDITED BY DAN DIAMOND

Previous page: The Red Wings took a 2–1 lead in the 1950 Stanley Cup Finals with a 4–0 win over the Rangers on April 15, 1950. The five heroes of that performance — left to right: Marty Pavelich, Sid Abel, Harry Lumley, Gerry Couture and George Gee — posed for the camera after the game. Pavelich scored the fourth and deciding goal and team captain Abel's unassisted marker with 44 seconds left in the second period gave the Red Wings a commanding 3–0 lead. Lumley shut out the New York attack, Couture scored the game winner on a powerplay and Gee's powerplay marker gave Detroit a 2–0 first-period advantage.

Facing Page: Photographed during the 1971 quarter-finals, superstars Bobby Orr and Henri Richard display the balance and co-ordination that separate hockey players from other athletes.

Canadian Cataloguing in Publication Data
Hockey Hall of Fame
         The spirit of the game: exceptional photographs from the Hockey Hall of Fame
Includes index.
ISBN: 0-394-22479-5

1. National Hockey League - Pictorial works.
2. Hockey - History - Pictorial works.
3. Hockey Hall of Fame - Photograph collections.
4. Photograph collections - Ontario - Toronto.
I. Diamond, Dan.   II. Title
GV846.5.H63 1995   796.962'022'2   C95-931179-3

Editor and Design: Dan Diamond
Photo Editor: Ralph Dinger
Research and Captions: James Duplacey
Coordinating Editor: Doug Pepper for Random House of Canada

Scanning and Film Production: Stafford Graphics, Toronto
Printed and bound in Canada on acid-free paper.

Published in the United States by:
Triumph Books
644 South Clark Street
Chicago, Illinois 60605
(312) 939-3330

95 96 97 98 99 00   1 2 3 4 5

For everyone who cares for the game

Hockey goes to war. After the Boston Bruins' Stanley Cup win in 1940–41, linemates Milt Schmidt, left, and Woody Dumart, right, joined the armed services and played hockey for the Royal Canadian Air Force Flyers. Under the direction of veteran NHL coach and manager Tommy "Tay-Pay" Gorman, seen here wearing a fedora at the center of the photo, the RCAF team captured the Allan Cup in 1941–42, giving both players a professional championship in 1941 and a senior amateur title in 1942.

Contents

Defenseman Allan Stanley, one of what Toronto coach Punch Imlach referred to as his "old pappies," cuts off Phil Esposito's path to the net during the 1967 semi-finals. By continuously forcing the Black Hawk forwards to veer away from the Leaf net, Stanley and the rest of Toronto's defenders were able to keep the Hawks at a distance. Although Chicago peppered the Leafs net with shots, many were from well out. Toronto, which finished the regular season 22 points behind the first-place Blackhawks, recorded the Stanley Cup playoff upset of the decade, eliminating Chicago in six games. The Leafs went on to win the Stanley Cup, defeating the Montreal Canadiens in a six-game final series.

THE CLICK OF THE CAMERA

INTRODUCTION
by Milt Dunnell

THIS IS WHAT HAPPENS when Dan Diamond sits down and shakes out what he considers to be the finest and most representative of an estimated five hundred thousand "images" (as in photographic prints and transparencies) from the collection of the Hockey Hall of Fame.

Hockey's blinding speed, its unique skills, its fury and its finesse, its beauty and its bruises, already have been portrayed by Diamond, via hundreds of thousands of words in volumes that recognized the seventy-fifth anniversary of the National Hockey League and the Stanley Cup's centennial.

In addition, Diamond produces the annual *NHL*

Official Guide & Record Book, generally recognized among professional sports organizations as the finest book of its kind.

Now, heeding the old adage that a picture is worth a thousand words, he happily accepts the gargantuan task of offering more than one hundred years of hockey history as recorded by the click of a camera.

He is prepared for differences of opinion. There is at least one indelible picture etched in the memory bank of every hockey fan.

Was it Bill Barilko's winning goal against Montreal Canadiens in the 1951 Stanley Cup final? Or did that image refuse to fade because Barilko disappeared on a fishing flight into the far northland a few weeks later, leaving his last goal as an epitaph?

Red Fisher, the Hall of Fame writer for the Montreal *Gazette*, undoubtedly has seen more hockey games than any other Canadian, alive or departed.

He was overwhelmed when asked to pick the single hockey picture that flashes instantly into his mind but he was willing to name one or two or three unforgettables. It's the image of Bobby Orr, flying past the St. Louis Blues' net, horizontal to the ice, after having delivered the winning shot of the 1970 Stanley Cup final, in the split second before Noel Picard of the Blues tripped him.

That picture is not in the Hall of Fame collection, but a companion piece does appear here. Shot by a fan sitting behind the St. Louis goal, it shows the puck entering the net behind Glenn Hall and Picard's stick wrapped around Orr's ankle just before launching him on his historic flight.

• • •

PICTORIALLY, hockey was the victim of its own speed and mobility. Photographers of the game's early years did not have the fast film and bright lights with which today's camera artists are blessed. Consequently, most of the

Bobby Orr's Cup-winning goal in 1970 as photographed from behind the St. Louis net. The puck is visible through the mesh just to the right of the goal frame's center bar.

Montreal Victorias, junior champions of Canada in 1896–97, featured a 16-year-old who would eventually become one of the game's first superstars. Russell Bowie (bottom row, second from right) won five scoring championships, scored at least five goals in a game 18 times and collected a career total of 234 goals in only 80 scheduled games.

early hockey art (to use a photo editor's term) was in the form of posed still pictures.

The top players of the day were lined up like shoppers at the cash counter in a supermarket, with their thatches and moustaches neatly combed and their teeth bared in pearly grins. The teeth were likely to be as phony as the poses. Most players lost their front teeth while still playing amateur hockey.

"Our research indicates that it wasn't until 1932–33 that action shots of hockey games began appearing with any kind of regularity in the daily papers of big cities," Diamond advises.

"The quality of these shots was very poor. So, while we sought out early action shots for this book, we have also included groups and posed still shots of players that have special significance for hockey."

Players kissing the Stanley Cup may not put stars in the eyes of sports editors but it was a different story when Terry Sawchuk and Sid Abel did it after the final game of the 1951–52 Cup capers. With Sawchuk showing the way, the Red Wings wrapped up the entire show in eight games, sweeping both playoff rounds in the tough six-team NHL. Sawchuk treated delirious Olympia fans to four consecutive shutouts. After that performance, Sawchuk was a front page picture just tying his shoelaces—especially in Detroit.

A picture that put a different tug on the heart strings also was a "still" that showed Toe Blake, club bag in hand, leaving the Montreal Forum in 1968. He had just won the Cup for the eighth time as a coach but there was no sense of joy in the picture. Blake announced his resignation the next day, ending the most successful coaching career in NHL history.

Ironically, Rocket Richard, whom the cameras captured hundreds of times barrelling in from the right rail for a shot on the net, doesn't even have the puck in a picture that is most likely to be republished today.

It's a million-to-one shot from the Turofsky collection that shows the glass being shattered by the impact of the Rocket's skate, after he was upended in a game at Maple Leaf Gardens. Richard is landing on the ice and Vic Lynn of the Leafs is caught watching the action over his shoulder.

Given the camera equipment of the day, it was a photographer's dream come true—all of the elements of the incident in place for the duration of a heartbeat.

The Turofsky brothers, Lou and Nat, were

Toronto's Vic Lynn, at left, looks on in disbelief as Montreal's Maurice Richard shatters a pane of "unbreakable" glass at Maple Leaf Gardens during the 1948–49 season.

among the country's best-known sports photographers. Nat did hockey, baseball and football. Lou, with his inevitable cigar, was as much a fixture as the quarter-pole at the race tracks.

In the early years of Maple Leaf Gardens, they had a contract to provide Leaf pictures to any legitimate publication that requested them. They also had an understanding with Conn Smythe, fiery owner of the Leafs, that they owed Smythe one of his trademark light gray felt hats any time they sent out a picture that showed an empty seat at a Leaf home game. There's no record of

April 21, 1951. A triumphant Bill Barilko is carried from the ice by Cal Gardner, left, and Bill Juzda after scoring the Stanley Cup-winning goal against the Montreal Canadiens in the Finals.

Bill Barilko around the Gardens after the winning goal in 1951."

Juzda also appears standing beside coach Joe Primeau at the Stanley Cup presentation. Most of the Leaf players are clustered around the trophy. Just a routine presentation shot, you're ready to huff. Not quite. The smiling Primeau has just completed a trifecta as coach of Memorial Cup (junior), Allan Cup (senior), and Stanley Cup (NHL) winners. Try to think of another coach who has done that—or is likely to.

Once photo editors commenced demanding on-ice action photos, photographers were ready to risk life and

how many historic shots fell victim to this arrangement.

Bill Juzda, then a hardhitting Leaf defenceman, now a retired gentleman golfer in Winnipeg, feels he was cheated by the camera. He claims it was he who sent the Rocket into orbit but he had moved out of range at the instant Richard's skate hit the glass.

"Caught him with my hip," Juzda insists. "A picture I also like to remember is me lugging

limb to provide them. Red Kelly, who played on eight Stanley Cup winners—four with the Red Wings and then, after his career was supposed to have ended, four more with the Leafs—recalls how Scotty Kilpatrick, a legendary photographer in Detroit, acquired one of his most memorable shots.

"Scotty apparently wanted something a little different, I guess," Kelly suggests, "so he crawled out on the girders, high over the ice at the Olympia. He got his picture—a great one—but he couldn't seem to get turned around for the return trip, with his equipment and everything. The Olympia staff had to send up a couple of guys to assist him."

Kelly, who had very few fistic encounters during his Hall of Fame career, still leans toward a fight between Gordie Howe and Lou Fontinato of the New York Rangers as the incident that provided his most memorable hockey pictures.

"Maybe it was because I was kind of involved," he suggests with a chuckle. "Eddie Shack was giving me a massage with his stick. Gordie saw I was having trouble getting Shackie off my back. When he moved in to lend a hand, that brought Fontinato into it. Shackie and I had ringside seats."

Red Kelly witnessed the Fontinato-Howe incident midway through a remarkable career that saw him win four Stanley Cup titles with Detroit and four more with Toronto.

IT TOOK THE ARRIVAL OF TELEVISION at NHL arenas to make just about everyone realize how poorly the rinks had been lighted. One of the first things television demanded was extra banks of lights.

"That improved things for us, too," Hal Barkley recalls. "Around 1942, I started shooting color action for the old *Star Weekly* (now long gone) using strobe lights, which we would pin up on the glass near the goal.

"When the TV guys first moved in, they used to complain that the flash of our lights when we took a shot created a momentary flicker in their picture, but this was something they were able to overcome. We really were grateful to them for the improved lighting."

Barkley remembers few protests from the fans concerning the strobe flashes, although one Chicago Stadium client did dump a cup of beer from an upper seat onto his equipment. He's inclined to excuse the guy for being drunk or maybe just frustrated because the Black Hawks were having a bad night.

"The beer caused a short circuit," Barkley says. "There was a tremendous bang and a brilliant flash, but no great commotion. That's about the only trouble I recall."

The players took the strobes in stride, too. Goaltending great Jacques Plante, then with the Maple Leafs, did protest one night, early in a game at the Montreal Forum. Referee Frank Udvari ordered that Barkley cease shooting.

Between periods, Barkley had a chance to speak to Jacques, who said that the only time the flash bothered him was when the ice was fresh and unscarred by skates. Once it became cut up a bit, there was no problem. Barkley promised there would be no flashes in the early minutes of a game or at the start of a period.

Plante was meticulous about possible employment hazards. At one time, when he

was with the Canadiens, he bailed out of the club's regular hotel in Toronto, claiming there was something about the furnishings that aggravated his allergies. He probably had it right but, at the time, was ridiculed.

Frank Prazak had another type of problem during the fifteen years he toured the NHL, shooting action and player portraits for *Weekend Magazine*, which appeared as a supplement in many Canadian dailies.

"There were things to be learned in each arena," he explains. "For instance, I set up one morning for a game that night in the old Madison Square Garden. When I returned for the game, I discovered that my sync cord had been cut.

"The sync cord was the long cable that connected the camera to the strobe lights which were right up in the rafters. I knew I had taken care of the electrician who had been there in the morning with a small bribe. What I didn't know was that the afternoon guy also expected to be kept happy. It cost me an extra

Arnie Brown (4) looks back in anger as this shot eludes the clutch of Jacques Plante in the New York Rangers cage. Ron Murphy (12), Jim Neilson (5) and Floyd Smith (17) are the other interested observers. Goals such as these sealed Plante's fate with the Rangers and the six-time Vezina Trophy winner was eventually sent to the minors to finish the season with the AHL's Baltimore Clippers.

fifty dollars but the important thing was that I got my pictures."

That always was the important thing—getting the pictures—and some of the best sports photographers in the business set the table, as they say in baseball, for later giants with state of the art equipment.

Dan Diamond has the best of both worlds. He has been free to pick from the feats of the modern millionaires—Gretzky, Lindros, Messier, Gilmour—and the Renfrew Millionaires—Lester Patrick, Sprague and Odie Cleghorn, and Cyclone Taylor.

In between those eras, there has been a lot of great reading. Now, here's a lot of great looking. ✦

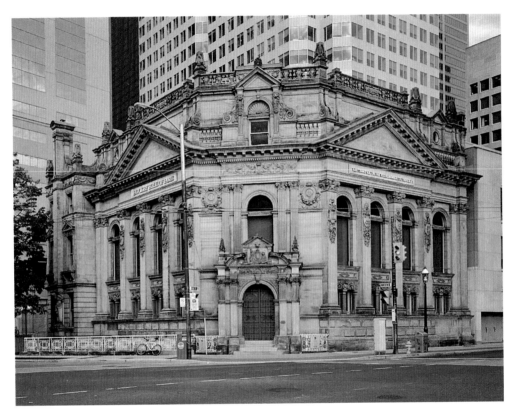

THE HOCKEY HALL OF FAME
• Staff •

Chairman: Ian Morrison • President: A. David M. Taylor
Vice-President, Operations: Jeffrey D. Denomme • Vice-President, Marketing: Bryan Black
Executive Assistant: Cindy Holloway • Manager: Facility Sales: Susan J. Bolender
Facility Sales Associate: Sally McIntyre • Manager, Operations & Services: M. Scott North
Special Events Co-ordinator: Janice McCabe • Education & Group Program Co-ordinator: Ron Ellis
Manager, Resource Centre & Acquisitions: Philip Pritchard • Marketing Manager: Christine Simpson
Manager, Facility Systems & Exhibit Development: Ray Paquet
Archivist & Research Specialist: Jefferson Davis
Assistant Manager, Resource Centre & Acquisitions: Craig Campbell
Manager, Guest Services: Christena Bozanis • Centre of Excellence Co-ordinator: Rick Morocco
Group Bookings Co-ordinator: Karyn Lisa Knott • Marketing Co-ordinator: Craig Baines
Special Events Co-ordinator: Andrew Bergant • Manager, Maintenance Services: Barry Eversley
Manager, Retail and Merchandise: Bryan McDermott • Accounting Supervisor: Sandra Buffone
Accountant: Sylvia Lau • Accountant Clerk: Anita Goel
Customer & Office Services Co-ordinator: Marilyn Robbins • Facility Services Assistant: Raymond Bruce
Receptionist: Pearl Rajwanth • Photographer: Doug MacLellan

ABOUT THE SPIRIT OF THE GAME

EDITOR'S NOTE

THE HOCKEY HALL OF FAME was established in 1943 and inducted its first honored members in 1945. In August of 1961, it opened its doors to the public in a building located on the grounds of the Canadian National Exhibition in Toronto. The Hall moved to its present site at BCE Place on the corner of Front and Yonge streets in downtown Toronto in June of 1993. In addition to housing the game's largest collection of artifacts and high-tech exhibitry, today's Hockey Hall of Fame is endowed with a well-stocked library that includes hockey's leading collection of archival photos.

This photo collection — all 500,000 images of it — was the resource from which *The Spirit of the Game* was created. The entire archive was examined, discussed and sifted through again and again to select the images that appear on the pages that follow. During this admittedly pleasant process, it became apparent that before a final photo selection could be completed, we had to resolve one big issue: was this book a historical document of record or was it a multi-layered picture of the game that evokes the passion invested in it?

In the end, the title tells all: we came down on the side of emotion. *The Spirit of the Game* celebrates those qualities that make hockey matter to its fans and participants. It takes you onto the ice and into the dressing room, spanning more than one hundred years of hockey as it does so. It is a book full of detail about how hockey has changed from players' equipment to broadcast technology, from the rules of the game to the fans in the seats.

It also is suffused with the joy and quiet satisfaction of heroes who've done their jobs and with players who gave their all, even if the numbers on the scoreboard don't reflect the desired result. *The Spirit of the Game* is divided into two parts. "The Spirit" deals with hockey's defining qualities, from kids to superstars, from courage to the Stanley Cup. "The Game" sweeps through a photographic history of the sport from the 1920s to today.

Within the Hockey Hall of Fame's archives, four photo collections provide the majority of pictures in *The Spirit of the Game.*

The Imperial Oil Turofsky collection contains the work of brothers Lou and Nat Turofsky. From 1909 to the early 1960s, the Turofskys were unmatched in their coverage of the Canadian sporting scene. Their cameras documented the first games played in Maple Leaf Gardens and went on to record many of the greatest moments in Maple Leafs history. Almost all of the Turofskys' work was shot in black-and-white.

Graphic Artists Studio led by Joe Black began photographing games at Maple Leaf Gardens in 1962, just as the eras of Conn Smythe and the Turofskys were drawing to a close. Working in both black-and-white and color, Graphic Artists continued the Turofsky legacy and also provided portrait services to other NHL clubs.

Frank Prazak began covering hockey for Montreal-based *Weekend Magazine* in the early 1960s. He shot some of the sport's first high-quality color action, covering the end of the six-team era, the early years of expansion and the first great international challenges between the best players in Europe and the NHL.

Doug MacLellan is the staff photographer at today's Hockey Hall of Fame. His work has given the Hall a contemporary color photo collection that documents the NHL as well as international, junior, college and women's hockey.

Most of the photos in this book were shot in Maple Leaf Gardens or the Montreal Forum, reflecting the home bases of the contributing photographers. The Turofskys, Graphic Artists and Frank Prazak all worked in the 1960s, so this decade is particularly well documented.

Many, many thanks to all who contributed their best work to *The Spirit of the Game.*

— *Dan Diamond*

When this photo of indoor hockey action was taken in 1893, the game was played with seven men per side, primitive equipment and two poles stuck in the ice to mark the goal. By the time the National Hockey League was formed in 1917, the game looked substantially different. Interestingly, the face-off formation shown in this image — players with their backs to the side boards — remained in vogue in the NHL until the 1942–43 season.

SECTION ONE

THE

SPIRIT

▼

Stan Mikita and Norm Ullman, two of the NHL's dominant centers in the 1960s, square off in the face-off circle with referee Vern Buffey during the 1964–65 season. Although referees only drop the puck at the start of a period or after goals in today's game, it was customary for the referee to drop the puck following off-sides or icings in the 1960s.

▶

Boston's Adam Oates has developed into one of the League's finest playmaking centers, reaching the 50-assist mark in six of his ten NHL seasons. Signed as a free agent by Detroit in 1985, he was traded to St. Louis in 1989. He earned a Second Team All-Star berth after an 115-point season with the Blues in 1990–91. He led the NHL with 97 assists in 1992–93.

The Montreal Amateur Athletic Association, or the "Winged Wheelers" as they were commonly called, were hockey's first dynasty team, winning the Amateur Hockey Association championship every year between 1886 and 1892. Five of this squad's seven members were still with the club when it was awarded the first Stanley Cup in 1893.

◀▼
Since the late 1980s, increased arena security and higher protective glass around the rink have allowed teams to celebrate their Stanley Cup victory on the ice with minimal interference from invading fans. It is now customary for teams to slowly parade around the ice, passing hockey's Holy Grail from player to player. In another modern Stanley Cup tradition, members of the Cup-winning team gather on the ice and pose for an informal team photo with the spoils of their victory. Here, the 1993 Montreal Canadiens surround a barely visible Stanley Cup after the Habs captured their 24th playoff championship.

▼
NHL president Clarence Campbell, at right, and members of the Stanley Cup champion Montreal Canadiens gather on the steps of Montreal's City Hall after a civic reception to honor the team in April 1956. Thirteen of the men who stood on the steps that day would later be inducted into the Hockey Hall of Fame: Jean Beliveau, Toe Blake, Butch Bouchard, Clarence Campbell, Bernie Geoffrion, Doug Harvey, Tom Johnson, Dickie Moore, Bert Olmstead, Jacques Plante, Henri Richard, Maurice Richard, and Frank Selke, Sr.

▶ The 1899–1900 Winnipeg Victorias, led by captain Dan Bain, goaltender George "Whitey" Merritt and winger Tony Gingras, lost a hard-fought best-of-three series to the Montreal Shamrocks in February 1900. After a 4–3 win in the opening contest, the Vics dropped 3–2 and 5–4 decisions to the Shamrocks.

◀ This 1906 Kenora Thistles team, which eventually went on to defeat the Montreal Wanderers for the Stanley Cup in January 1907, included future Hall-of-Famers Si Griffis (front, left), Tom Phillips (front, right), Tom Hooper (center) and Billy McGimsie (back, right).

◀ The newly-formed Toronto Blueshirts entered the National Hockey Association during the 1912–13 season and compiled a 9–11 record in their first season. With future Hall-of-Fame members Harry "Hap" Holmes, Frank Foyston, Frank Nighbor and Harry Cameron on board, the Blueshirts went on to the raise their first Stanley Cup banner in 1914.

◀ The Toronto St. Pats pose beside Mutual Street Arena prior to the start of the 1926–27 season. When Conn Smythe and his group of investors purchased the team on Valentine's Day, 1927, and renamed them the Toronto Maple Leafs, Smythe chose future Hall-of-Famers Ace Bailey (back row, second from left) and Hap Day (front row, third from left) to form the nucleus of the new squad.

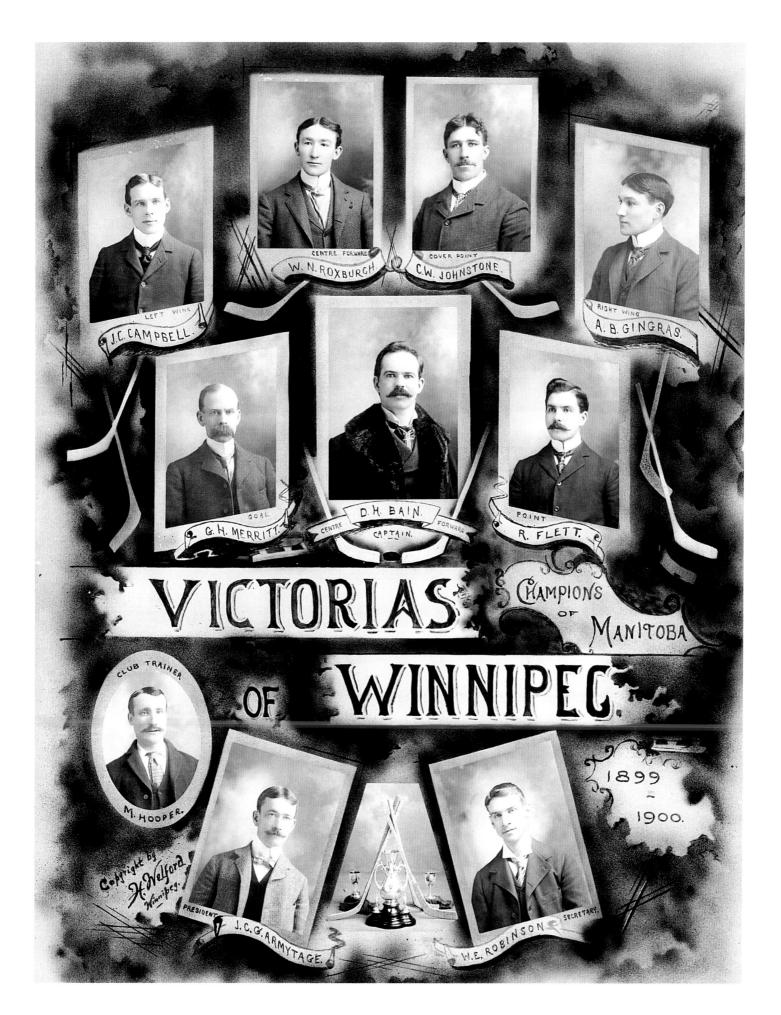

In 1932, American industrialist James Norris, Sr. bought the Detroit Falcons franchise and renamed the team the Red Wings, adopting a winged wheel as the franchise logo. Norris imported the symbol from Canada, where he had played for the Montreal AAA's Winged Wheelers. Two years after Norris bought the club, the Red Wings advanced to the Stanley Cup Finals, only to lose in four games to the Chicago Black Hawks.

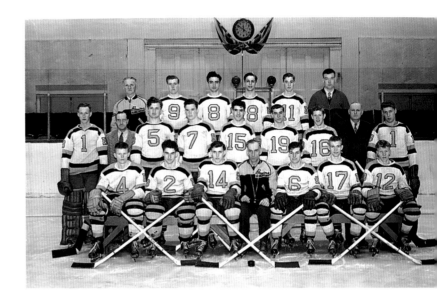

Detroit Red Wings 1933-34—National Hockey League Champions

◀
This 1947–48 Port Arthur West End Bruins team swept the Barrie Flyers in four straight games to become the first team from the Lakehead to win the Memorial Cup. The team, which featured future NHL players such as Danny Lewicki, Benny Woit, and Dave Creighton, also included goaltender Lorne Chabot Jr., (far right, second row) the son of the beetle-browed great who backstopped the Port Arthur team to consecutive Allan Cup senior amateur titles in 1924 and 1925.

▼
The Conn Smythe Trophy awarded to the MVP in each year's playoffs sits in front of general manager Bill Torrey in this team portrait of the Cup-winning New York Islanders of 1981. Center Butch Goring, top row at right, played superb two-way hockey and recorded 20 playoff points to win the award. Many analysts consider Goring to have been the last piece of the puzzle needed to launch the Islanders' four-year Cup dynasty.

This outdoor scrimmage by the Detroit Falcons took place during training camp prior to the 1931–32 season. While skating, checking and passing drills are designed to improve skill levels, coaches still depend on inter-squad scrimmages to determine which of their players have the mettle to excel in the world's fastest game.

◄
The "Major" Conn Smythe, far right, looks on as he puts his troops through their paces during a Toronto Maple Leafs training camp in 1932. While exercise and stretching routines remain an integral part of pre-season training to this day, it's doubtful that today's players are required to complete their push-ups in the middle of a gravel road in full equipment.

▶
Referee Francis "King" Clancy helps an obviously bloodied and shaken Jimmy Orlando off the ice after the Red Wing tough guy and Toronto forward Gaye Stewart had a prolonged stick-swinging duel during Toronto's 5–2 win over Detroit on November 7, 1942. The game marked the first meeting between the two teams since the Leafs' dramatic comeback from a 3–0 deficit in the 1942 Stanley Cup Finals.

◄
Bernie Geoffrion is led off the ice after spraining his wrist in a goalmouth scramble during a 2–1 victory over the Toronto Maple Leafs on December 5, 1962. Geoffrion, who only played one complete season in his 16-year NHL career, missed almost two weeks of action because of the resulting sore wrist.

▲
Brad May is attended by the Buffalo Sabres training staff during the 1991–92 season. In the first 50 years of the NHL's existence, the assistant trainer was usually a practice goalie whose skills were more inclined to taping sticks than nursing injuries. Many of today's head trainers and assistants hold degrees in physiotherapy and sports medicine.

◀
The Walking Wounded. Doug Gilmour's heroic journey through the 1993 Stanley Cup playoffs is the stuff of legends. Despite being battered and bloodied, Gilmour's inspirational play and 35 points in 21 games lifted the Maple Leafs into the NHL's final four for the first time in 15 years.

▲

Doug Gilmour, left, attempts to strong-arm Detroit defenseman Mark Howe off the puck during this spirited Red Wing–Maple Leaf tilt on February 20, 1995. No Detroit Red Wing team has won the Stanley Cup without there being a player named Howe in the lineup. Mark's father, Gordie, played on four Cup-winners in the 1950s. Syd Howe — no relation — was on a Cup winner in 1936, 1937 and 1943.

▶

Until the 1960s, only the ends of the rink and the corners were protected with wire mesh or unbreakable glass, meaning that action along the sides of the rink was often hectic and dangerous for fans. Here, a row of spectators covers up as Detroit defenseman Bob Goldham squeezes Toronto's Jim Morrison into the boards during the 1952–53 season. Morrison is wearing the "C" for the Leafs, having inherited the captain's mantle after Ted Kennedy broke his collar bone in a game against Boston on January 1, 1953.

On November 16, 1991, less than a month after being acquired by the Buffalo Sabres from the New York Islanders, Pat LaFontaine fractured his jaw during a 5–4 victory over Calgary. After nursing the injury for 13 games, LaFontaine returned to action wearing a specially designed helmet, face shield and jaw protector.

▶
New York Americans' defenseman Peter Slobodzian wore this wire cage during the 1940–41 season, the only NHL campaign of his career.

▼
Defenseman Marcel Pronovost of the Detroit Red Wings models a crude but effective face shield to protect a broken nose he suffered during the 1955–56 season. Injuries to a number of key forwards forced coach Jimmy Skinner to move Red Kelly from the blueline to the forward line in December 1955. Kelly played 26 games as a forward, but moved back to defense when Pronovost was injured.

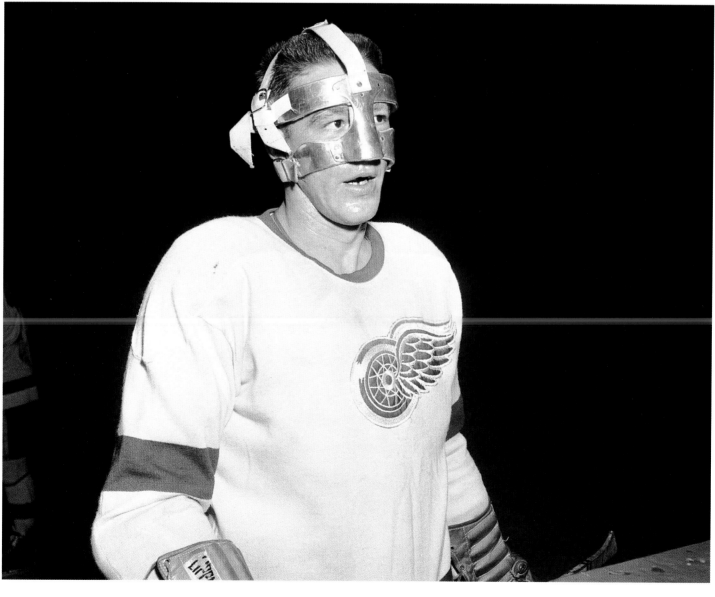

▶

Wandering goaltender Doug Favell gets caught out of position, much to the surprise of Philadelphia defenders Bob Sutherland (11) and Joe Watson. Favell stayed in the crease long enough to stop 45 shots as the Flyers snuck past the frustrated Maple Leafs 2–1 in this January 24, 1968, contest.

▼

Luckily, neither Rod Gilbert (7) nor Phil Goyette of the Rangers were seriously injured when they were knocked down by Eddie Shack during New York's 6–3 loss to Toronto on December 19, 1965. This was one of the few breaks that went Goyette's way during the season. He opened the campaign with a nagging wrist injury and ended with a serious case of bronchitis, forcing him to miss 18 games.

It's doubtful that Detroit goaltender Terry Sawchuk enjoyed this performance by Eddie "The Entertainer" Shack during the 1963–64 season. A bandy-legged whirling dervish on skates, Shack was an aggressive pest whose rare combination of physical force and scoring skill made him a crowd favorite in Maple Leaf Gardens.

▼
The last Hall-of-Fame goaltender to play without a mask, Lorne "Gump" Worsley crawls back to the safety of his crease after a close call during the 1970–71 campaign. Worsley shunned the security of the facemask until September 23, 1973, when he wore one in an exhibition game against Toronto. After the North Stars downed the Leafs 5–4, the Gumper decided to wear the mask for the rest of the season.

▶
In this early version of on-ice synchronized spinning, Harry Watson, left, and his New York Ranger dance partner show excellent form as they both hit the deck with sticks at the proper angle, leverage on their leg kicks and just the right facial grimace.

◄

Gerry James of the Toronto Maple Leafs makes a three-point landing after being tripped up by Chicago's Pierre Pilote during first-period action in the Leafs' 1–0 victory over the Black Hawks on March 19, 1960. James undoubtedly preferred the kind of three-point plays he routinely made as a place kicker for football's Winnipeg Blue Bombers where he also earned All-Star berths as a halfback in 1957 and 1958. James was a true two-sport athlete, playing five seasons with the Leafs as an abrasive right winger on the club's third line.

▼

Boston defenseman Gilles Marotte performs a nicely choreographed move to avoid a collision with goaltender Ed Johnston as Dave Keon and the puck slide toward the vacated net. Toronto threw everything at the Boston net on this evening, including 50 shots, as the Leafs ushered in the new year with a 6–3 victory over the Bruins on January 1, 1966.

◀

A pensive Dick Irvin reflects on his success as the head coach of the Toronto Maple Leafs, a post he held for nine seasons from 1931–32 to 1939–40. Irvin, who began his coaching career in Chicago, joined the Montreal organization in 1941 and guided the Canadiens into the Stanley Cup finals eight times.

▼

The blackboard, the champagne, the Stanley Cup and the contented look on Punch Imlach's face give notice that the 1962–63 season ended as the club's clairvoyant coach and general manager had predicted, with the Maple Leafs winning it all.

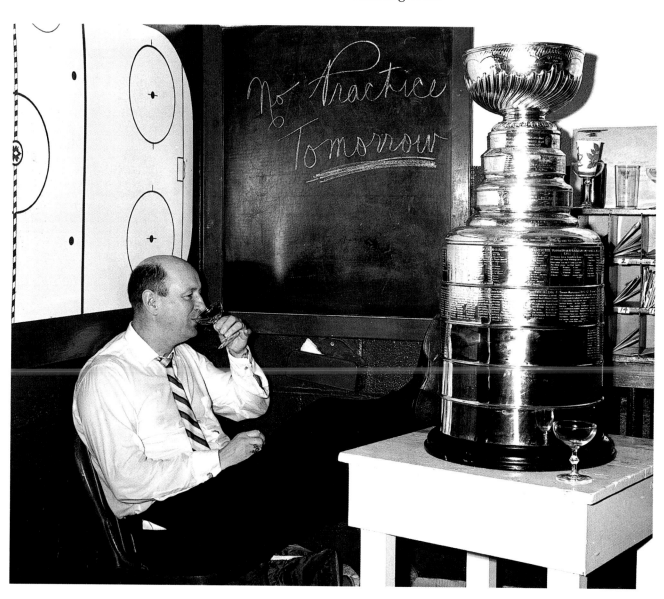

Hall-of-Fame forward Hector "Toe" Blake made his coaching debut with the Houston Huskies of the United States Hockey League after retiring as a player during the 1947–48 campaign when he was sidelined by a badly broken leg. Blake actually made a pair of on-ice comebacks in the minor leagues with the Buffalo Bisons in 1948–49 and the Valleyfield Braves in 1949–50. In 1955, he was appointed coach of the Montreal Canadiens. A driven man, tough and loyal to players who served the club well, the "Old Lamplighter" guided the Habs to eight Stanley Cup titles before retiring after the 1967–68 season. As this book was nearing completion, Blake passed away after a lenghty battle with Alzheimer's disease.

A nattily-attired Scotty Bowman barks out a few commands to his Montreal Canadien charges during a 9–2 loss to the Toronto Maple Leafs on December 26, 1973. Although the Habs took a beating on this evening, Bowman ranks first among NHL coaches with 913 career victories.

◀
Francis "King" Clancy's "luck o' the Irish" rubbed off on the Toronto Maple Leafs during his three-week term as Leaf coach during the 1966–67 season. After a disastrous month that saw the team lose 10 of 12 games, coach Punch Imlach succumbed to the strain and was hospitalized for exhaustion. The Leafs, who downed the Boston Bruins 5–3 in Clancy's debut on February 18, 1967, strung together a 10-game unbeaten streak with the King behind the bench.

◀
Sid Abel issues a few instructions to his Detroit Red Wing players during the 1960–61 season. Known as "Old Bootnose" during his 14-year playing career in Detroit and Chicago, Abel is the only coach in NHL history to reach the Stanley Cup finals four times without winning the championship.

▶ Al Arbour, a 14-year veteran who played on Stanley Cup-winning teams in Detroit, Chicago and Toronto, was the first captain of the St. Louis Blues. Named coach of the Blues prior to the start of the 1970–71 campaign, Arbour spent only 50 games behind the bench that season before returning to active duty on the Blues' blueline. He would later go on to coach the New York Islanders to four consecutive Stanley Cup championships beginning in 1980.

▶ Thirty-three-year-old rookie coach Harry Sinden watches intently as his Boston Bruins drop a 2–1 decision to the Toronto Maple Leafs on December 14, 1966. Sinden, who had coached the Kingston Frontenacs to the Eastern Pro League crown and piloted the Oklahoma City Bruins to the Central League title, was the youngest head coach in NHL history when he took over the reins of the struggling Boston franchise in June 1966.

◄ Bill Reay, seen here during the 1972–73 season, ranks fourth on the all-time games-coached register. Reay, who began his coaching career with the Toronto Maple Leafs in 1957 before joining the Chicago Black Hawks in 1963, retired in 1977 after working 1,102 games behind the bench.

▼ Fred "the Fog" Shero earned his nickname when he was playing with the St. Paul Saints of the United States Hockey League in 1947–48. After 13 seasons as a coach in such minor-league outposts as Buffalo and Omaha, Shero was named coach of the Philadelphia Flyers on June 2, 1971. He quickly molded the club into a hard-hitting, tight-checking unit that rode solid goaltending and timely scoring to a pair of Stanley Cup championships in the mid–1970s.

▶

Mike Keenan exorcised both his own demons and the New York Rangers' 54-year curse by guiding the club to its first Stanley Cup title since 1940. Keenan, who had lost previous title bids with Chicago and Philadelphia, jumped off the Rangers' bandwagon shortly after this victory photo was taken to join the St. Louis Blues as the club's coach and general manager.

▼

Barry Melrose, right, and assistant coach Cap Raeder watch the seconds tick down as the Los Angeles Kings fall victim to the Montreal Canadiens in the 1993 Stanley Cup Finals. A journeyman defenseman who patrolled the blueline for three different teams during his eight-year NHL career, Melrose guided the Medicine Hat Tigers to the Memorial Cup title and piloted the Adirondack Red Wings to the Calder Cup crown before taking over the Kings' throne in 1992.

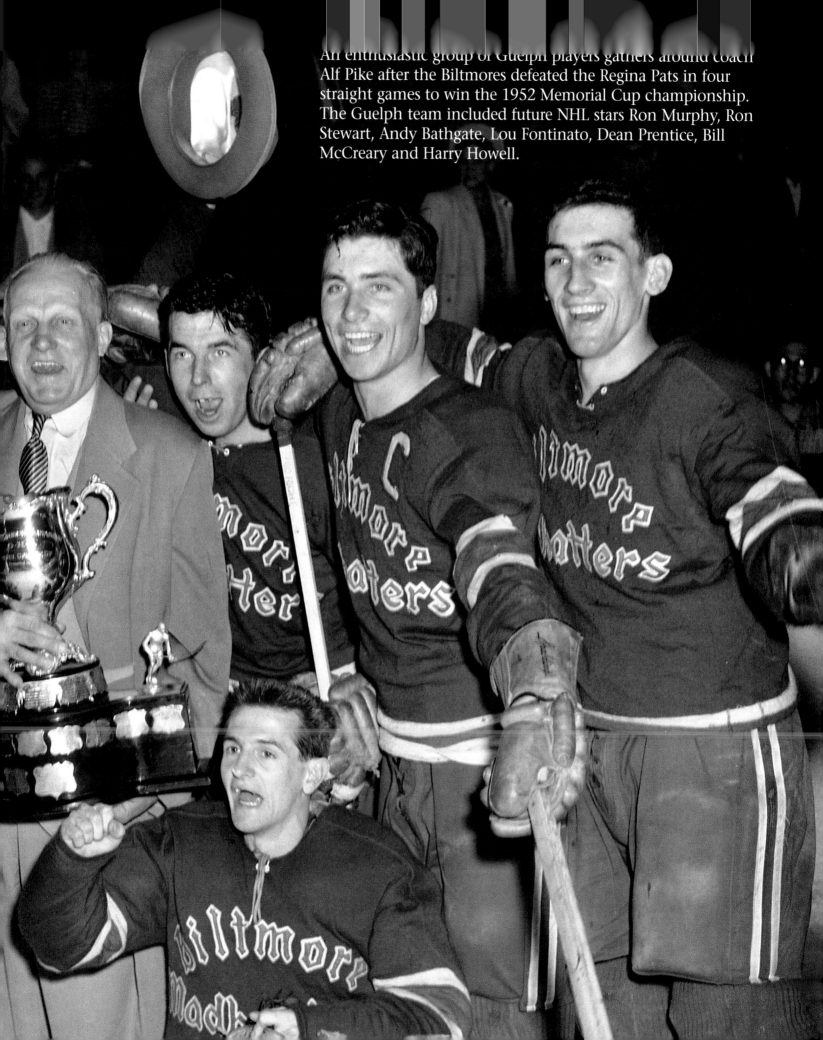

An enthusiastic group of Guelph players gathers around coach Alf Pike after the Biltmores defeated the Regina Pats in four straight games to win the 1952 Memorial Cup championship. The Guelph team included future NHL stars Ron Murphy, Ron Stewart, Andy Bathgate, Lou Fontinato, Dean Prentice, Bill McCreary and Harry Howell.

"Old Turkey Eyes," Walter "Turk" Broda has his hands full carting the Vezina Trophy home after his outstanding goaltending display during the 1947–48 season. Broda led all NHL netminders in wins (32), and goals-against average (2.38) as he interrupted Montreal All-Star Bill Durnan's four-year hold on the silverware.

◀
Harold Ballard, one of three co-owners of the Toronto Maple Leafs, proudly displays the Prince of Wales Trophy after the team clinched first place in 1962–63. The Leafs' 82-point record marked only the second time that the club finished first overall in the regular season, although they did finish atop the NHL's Canadian Division four times in the 1930s.

▶
Outstanding junior prospect Yvan Cournoyer poses with the Red Tilson Trophy after being named the Ontario Junior Hockey League's MVP in 1963–64. Known as "The Roadrunner," the speedy forward collected 63 goals and 111 points in leading the Montreal Junior Canadiens to a second-place finish in the OJHL.

▶

A first time for everything: Wayne Gretzky poses with the Art Ross Trophy and the Hart Trophy after capturing this matched pair of awards for the first time in the 1980–81 season. The Great One would carry home this combo platter seven times in his career.

▼

Prior to the opening game of 1964–65, NHL president Clarence Campbell presents three members of the Chicago Black Hawks with the silverware they won during the 1963–64 season. Pierre Pilote holds the Norris Trophy, Stan Mikita clutches the Art Ross while Kenny Wharram embraces the Lady Byng. Wharram, who suffered a badly broken nose in an exhibition game against Toronto, had to attend the opening game festivities in civvies.

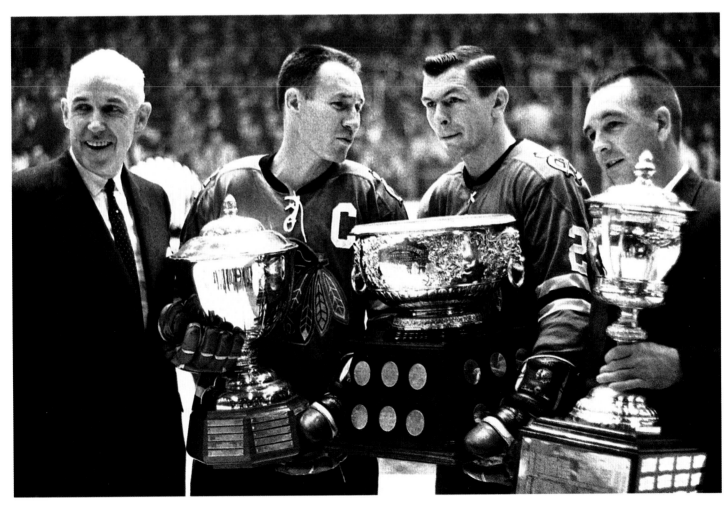

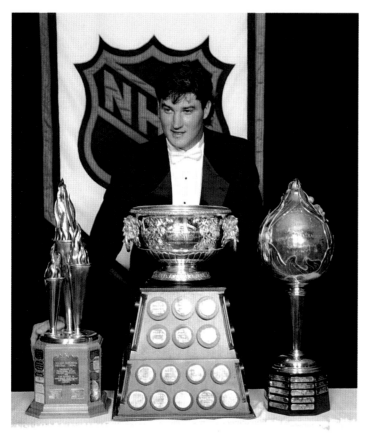

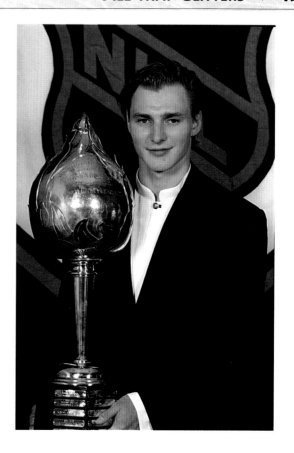

Despite missing 24 games due to injury and illness during the 1992–93 season, Mario Lemieux still managed to win the NHL scoring title, a feat that also earned him the Hart Trophy as MVP and the Masterton Trophy for perseverance and sportsmanship

The first European-trained player to win the Hart Trophy, Detroit's Sergei Fedorov had a spectacular season at both ends of the ice in 1993–94, adding the Selke Trophy for the best defensive forward to his MVP award.

Teemu Selanne rewrote the rookie record book in 1992–93, establishing NHL freshman marks for both goals (76) and points (132) for the Winnipeg Jets. In addition to receiving the Calder Trophy, Selanne earned a berth on both the NHL's First All-Star Team and All-Rookie Team.

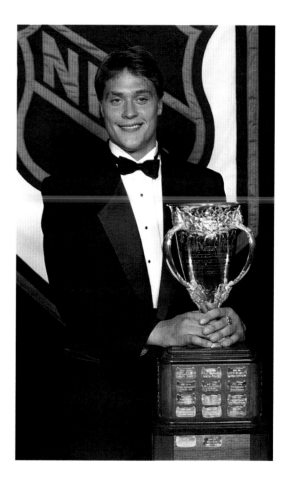

◄
The Whitby Dunlops were a star-studded senior squad that included manager Wren Blair, goaltender Roy Edwards, Sid Smith, Connie Broden and captain Harry Sinden. In 1957, the "Dunnies" won the Allan Cup and were invited to represent Canada at the 1958 IIHF World Hockey Championships. The Dunlops helped Canada regain the world amateur title by winning seven straight games, including a decisive 4–2 victory over the USSR in the last game of the tournament. Sports and politics were intertwined even in the 1950s: in 1957, Canada had withdrawn from the World Championships to protest the Soviet invasion of Hungary.

▼
Bob Forhan of the Canadian National Team sneaks a backhand past Swedish National Team goaltender Leif Holmqvist, helping Canada record a 6–3 victory over Sweden on December 29, 1963. The game, played in front of 10,111 fans at Maple Leaf Gardens, was part of a three-team, three-game round-robin tournament featuring the national teams of Canada, Sweden and Czechoslovakia.

▼
Canadian National Team defenders Wayne Stephenson (21) and Terry O'Malley (4) cover Soviet forward Vladimir Vikulov during Canada's 4–3 victory over the Soviet Union on January 10, 1967. It was the home side's third straight game without a loss during the defending IIHF World Champions' Canadian tour. Other results included a 5–4 Canadian win in Winnipeg and a 3–3 draw in Montreal.

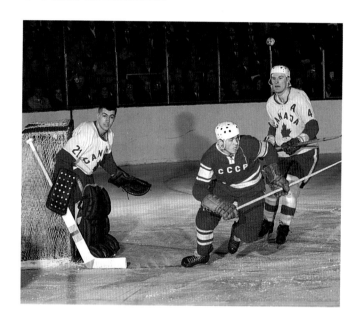

◀
In November 1957, a team of Russian Selects traveled to Canada for an eight-game exhibition tour against junior and senior clubs from Ontario and Quebec. The first game, played in front of a full house at Maple Leaf Gardens on November 22, 1957, featured a World Championship preview between the Russians and the Whitby Dunlops, who would later represent Canada at the 1958 World tournament. The Selects scored a pair of goals in the opening minutes to grab a quick 2–0 lead, but the Dunnies stormed back for seven unanswered goals to collect a 7–2 victory. Here, Charlie Burns sneaks the puck past the outstretched pad of Russian netminder Vladimir Puchkov to score the final goal in the decisive victory. The Selects finished their tour with a 5–2–1 record.

◄

Former NHL star Billy Harris (15) accelerates past a Czechoslovakian forechecker while goaltender Ken Dryden stands on guard during the Czech National Team's 4–0 victory over the Canadian National Team on January 1, 1970. The game was part of a five-game exhibition series between the two countries, and was supposed to be a tune-up for the 1970 IIHF World Championships which were scheduled for Winnipeg. As part of a new agreement with the IIHF, Canada's roster could include nine professional players, none of whom had played in the NHL in 1969–70. However, on January 3, 1970, the IIHF announced, "Any amateur team that competes against the Canadian professionals . . . will be stripped of its amateur status." This effectively ended Canada's hopes of using its best players. The next day, John Munro, the federal Minister of Health and Welfare, announced Canada's withdrawal from international hockey competition until professional players were eligible to compete. The 1970 Championships were shifted to Stockholm. This international hockey cold war endured until Canada returned to the IIHF World Championships in 1977.

◄

After watching the Soviet Nationals skate circles around Team Canada in the opening game of the 1972 Canada–Russia showdown, fans finally got an opportunity to see Team Canada's speed in action. Early in the third period of game two, Yvan Cournoyer took a pass from Brad Park and cruised through the Russian defense to score the go–ahead goal in an eventual 4-1 victory.

Team Canada's Tony Esposito gets tested in close by Russia's Valery Kharlamov during game two of the 1972 "Series of the Century." Although Tony "O" stoned Kharlamov on this occasion, the Soviet superstar collected seven points in the eight-game set, impressing fans around the world with his wide array of skating and shooting skills.

One of the most dramatic moments of the 1972 Canada–Russia series came early in the third period of game two. Team Canada, still reeling from a 7–3 thrashing in the opening match of the eight-game set, was clinging to a slim 2–1 advantage in game two when Bobby Clarke was sent to the penalty box for slashing. With the Russians flooding the Canadian zone, Phil Esposito picked up a loose puck along the boards and slipped an outlet pass to Peter Mahovlich at the Russian blueline. The "Little M" left Soviet defenseman Evgeni Padadiev grasping at air with a wonderfully executed fake slapshot, then pulled a marvellous deke on netminder Vladislav Tretiak before stuffing the insurance goal into the empty cage. Canada held on for a 4–1 victory, tying the "Summit Series" at one game apiece.

▼
The Soviet Union's "Superline" of Boris Mikhailov (13), Valery Kharlamov and Vladimir Petrov (16) pressures Team Canada's Pat Stapleton (12) and J.C. Tremblay (3) as goaltender Gerry Cheevers gets a toe on the puck during game two of the WHA/Russia series on September 19, 1974. In September and October of 1974, a team of Canadian-born all-stars from the World Hockey Association played an eight-game series against the Soviet National Team. The Canadian team, which included Frank Mahovlich, Paul Henderson and Stapleton from Team Canada '72, won the Toronto date on the tour 4–1 for its only victory of the series.

▶
Bobby Clarke muscles past Czech defender Jiri Novak during game one of the best-of-three final between Canada and Czechoslovakia in the inaugural Canada Cup tournament of 1976. The Canadians defeated a talented Czech squad 6–0 and 5–4 to capture the Canada Cup crown.

Bobby Orr (4), Bob Gainey (34), Larry Robinson (at left) and Gil Perreault (11) join in the on-ice melee as members of Team Canada celebrate Darryl Sittler's series-winning goal against Czechoslovakia in the 1976 Canada Cup final. Orr, who was forced to miss the 1972 Series of the Century because of a knee injury and played only ten games during the NHL's 1975–76 season, played the last great hockey of his career during the Canada Cup, winning the tournament's MVP award.

▲
One of the greatest upsets in hockey history was orchestrated by the United States Olympic Team at the 1980 Winter Games in Lake Placid. With coach Herb Brooks behind the bench and a top-notch crop of college athletes in the lineup, the U.S. amateurs downed the Soviet Union 4–3 and Finland 4–2 to capture the gold medal. Seventeen of the 27 players and coaches from this team, including Brooks, Neal Broten, Dave Christian, Mark Johnson, Ken Morrow, Mike Ramsey and Craig Patrick continued their hockey careers in the NHL.

▶
The first member of the Chicago Blackhawks to record three consecutive 100-point seasons, Jeremy Roenick has been a model of consistency since he joined the NHL late in the 1988–89 season. He played for Team USA in the 1991 Canada Cup tournament, leading the squad into the finals with four goals and six points in eight games.

EDMONTON MONARCHS. 1924-25.

Solloway-Mills & Company
Ladies. Hockey Team   Ottawa & District Champs 1928-29

◀

The Edmonton Monarchs hockey club, including the 1924–25 squad pictured here, was one of the most successful women's teams of the 1920s and 1930s. In 1927, the Monarchs lost their Alberta title in a 1–0 nail-biter to the Calgary Hollies, but regained the championship the following year, downing the Hollies by an identical 1–0 count.

◀▼

The all-women's Solloway Mills team was crowned as Ottawa city champion in 1928–29. The team then went on to meet the Toronto Pats for the Ladies' Ontario Hockey Association championship, but lost the two-game, total-goal series three goals to two. Goaltender Olive Barr was singled out as one of the most valuable players in the series.

▼

A joyous Canadian National Women's Team celebrates its third consecutive IIHF World title after downing Team USA 6–3 in the gold medal game in Lake Placid, New York, on April 17, 1994. The Canadian women, led by goaltender Manon Rheaume and team captain France St-Louis, finished the round-robin tournament with a 5–0 record, outscoring their opponents by an aggregate score of 37–7.

▼
The International Hockey League's Fort Wayne Comets and Phoenix Roadrunners do battle on January 16, 1993. Although it has been in operation since 1945, the IHL has only recently become a major player on the minor-league circuit, averaging 7,000 fans per game. By its 50th anniversary season of 1994–95, the "I" had grown to 17 teams, including clubs in current or former NHL cities such as Atlanta, Denver, Cleveland, Minnesota, Chicago and Detroit.

▶
Despite appearing in only one NHL game in his career, Donald S. Cherry is one of the game's best-known personalities. A career minor leaguer who played with nine different teams in five different leagues before becoming a successful coach in the both the AHL and the NHL, Cherry's current forum is Coach's Corner on Molson Hockey Night in Canada on CBC. With broadcaster Ron MacLean as his foil, the acid-tongued Cherry gives Canadians from coast-to-coast a state-of-the-game address every Saturday night during the regular season and more frequently during the playoffs.

▲

Journeyman center Jack Gordon spent four years in the New York Rangers organization before joining the American Hockey League's Cleveland Barons. He played ten seasons in Cleveland and served as the team's playing coach during the last six. After a five-year absence, Gordon returned to the Barons in 1968 as coach and general manager. In 1970, he was named coach of the Minnesota North Stars, a post he held until 1975.

◄

When he wrapped up his junior career with the Quebec Citadels in 1951, Jean Beliveau opted to sign with the Quebec Aces of the Quebec Senior Hockey League instead of joining the NHL's Montreal Canadiens. Beliveau is rumored to have earned as much playing with the Aces as the highest paid player in the NHL, making his decision to spend two seasons in the Quebec league a rather one-sided choice. Beliveau led the QSHL in scoring in both his seasons with the Aces and scored 50 goals in 1952–53, his final campaign with the team.

◄
An enthusiastic group of St. Mike's players gather in the dressing room after demolishing the Montreal Jr. Canadiens 21–0 in the final game of the 1947 Eastern Canada Memorial Cup showdown. The St. Mike's team featured goaltender Howie Harvey, defenseman Red Kelly (3), captain Ed Sanford (2), coach Joe Primeau (standing at right) and scoring hero Fleming Mackell (standing, second from right) who scored six goals in the record-setting victory. Primeau's team went on to defeat the Moose Jaw Canucks in four straight games to win the 1947 Memorial Cup title.

◄
Manager Matt Leyden, middle row at left, and coach Charlie Conacher, middle row, second from left, celebrate with their charges after the Oshawa Generals captured the Canadian Junior A hockey championship and the Memorial Cup in 1943–44. Team members included Dave Bauer, who would go on to become famous as Father David Bauer, founder of the Canadian National Team (bottom row, second from left), goaltender Harvey Bennett, Floyd "Busher" Curry (top row, third from left), Ted Lindsay (top row at right) and Gus Mortson (middle row, fourth from right).

▼
Coach Rudy Pilous and the St. Catharines TeePees celebrate after defeating the Edmonton Oil Kings in the fifth and deciding game of the 1954 Memorial Cup finals. The TeePees won the best-of-seven series with four wins (8–2, 5–3, 4–1, 6–2) and one tie (3–3) thanks in large part to the efforts of the CBC Line — Barry Cullen (10), Hugh Barlow (11) and Brian Cullen (14) — and goaltender Marv Edwards (1).

◀

Four members of the Edmonton Oil Kings — from left to right: Bobby Marik, Ed Joyal, Cliff Pennington and Bruce MacGregor — celebrate their 9–3 win over the St. Catharines Teepees in game four of the 1960 Memorial Cup finals. Ed Joyal led the attack with four goals, Pennington and MacGregor chipped in with two each and Marik added one more in the victory. Unfortunately for the Oil Kings, the Teepees captured the Canadian junior title in six games.

▼

The 1944–45 Moose Jaw Canucks pose in Maple Leaf Gardens prior to the start of the 1945 Memorial Cup championships. The Canucks, whose roster included coach Roy Bentley (standing, fourth from left), goaltender Bev Bentley, Bert Olmstead (front, second from right), and Metro Prystai (front, third from left), defeated Winnipeg to win the Western Canada junior title. Although they put up a brave fight against Toronto's St. Michael's College in the national finals, Moose Jaw dropped the best-of-seven series in five games.

▲
Alex Delvecchio as a member of the Oshawa
Generals during the 1950–51 season, his final
year in junior. The following season, Delvecchio
was promoted to the Detroit Red Wings after only
six games of minor-league tutoring in the AHL.
"Fats" went on to 24 years in the NHL, retiring in
1973–74.

▶
Edmonton Oil Kings defender Glen Sather can't
prevent this backhander from entering the empty
cage to give the Toronto Marlboros a commanding
lead in game four of the 1964 Memorial Cup finals.
The Marlies, a powerhouse team that included Ron
Ellis, Pete Stemkowski and Rod Seiling, swept the
finals in four straight games.

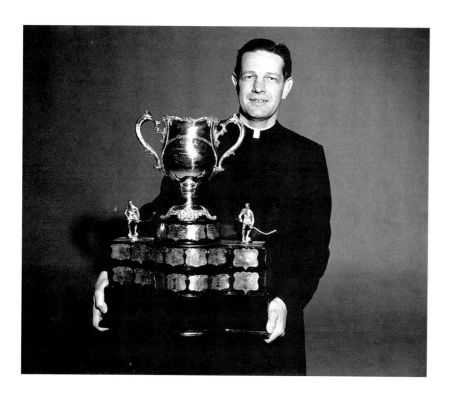

The architect of the Canadian National Team program, Father David Bauer, poses with the Memorial Cup after his St. Michael's College team captured the Canadian junior championship in 1961. The following season, St. Mike's dropped out of Memorial Cup competition and Father Bauer turned his attention to organizing a program that would mix university education with athletics. The National Team concept was born.

▼

Members of the Toronto Marlboros, including Ron Ellis, Wayne Carleton, Rod Seiling, Pete Stemkowski, Brit Selby, Barry Watson, Mike Walton and Gary Dineen, celebrate gaining a berth in the 1964 Memorial Cup championships after defeating the Montreal Notre Dame de Grace Monarchs 11–3 on May 1, 1964. The Marlies, who won the best-of-five round in four games, got hat-tricks from Pete Stemkowski and Wayne Carleton and a two-goal effort from Jack Chipchase in the decisive victory over the Monarchs.

▶

Like most goaltenders of his era, Edmonton Oil Kings netminder Russ Gillow plays through pain after taking a shot above the eye during the 1964 Memorial Cup championships series against the Marlies. Gillow would later spend four seasons in the World Hockey Association with the Los Angeles Sharks and the San Diego Mariners.

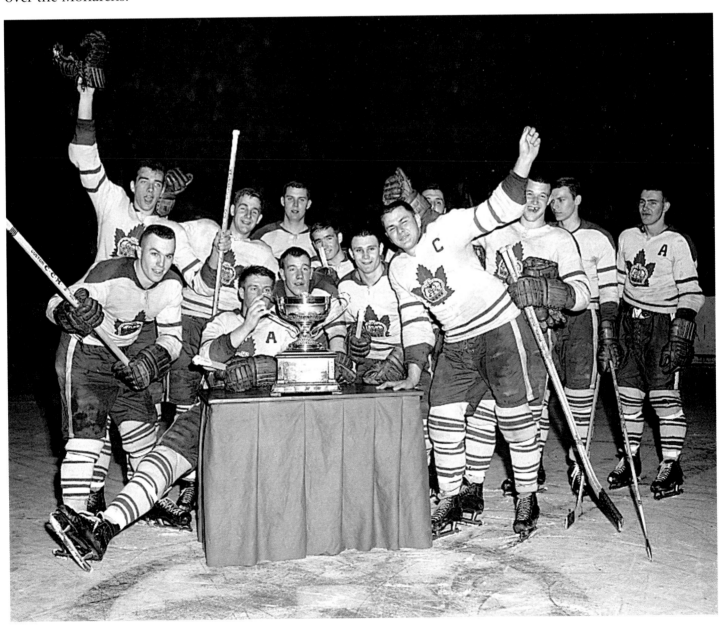

◄

Chris Pronger, seen here playing for the OHL/WHL All-Stars in the Canadian Hockey League All-Star Game on January 19, 1993. Pronger, who would go on to be drafted second overall in the 1993 Entry Draft by the Hartford Whalers, picked up an assist as the combined Western and Ontario League All-Stars defeated their Quebec counterparts 7–5.

▼

Dale Hawerchuk, right, and Winnipeg Jets general manager John Ferguson model a Jets jersey after Winnipeg selected Hawerchuk first overall in the 1981 Entry Draft. Hawerchuk, a graduate of the Cornwall Royals, was the Canadian Major Junior Player of the Year in 1981 after compiling 183 points in 72 games. Hawerchuk won rookie-of-the-year honors the following season, lifting the Jets from a 9–57–14 record in 1980–81 to the .500 mark in 1981–82.

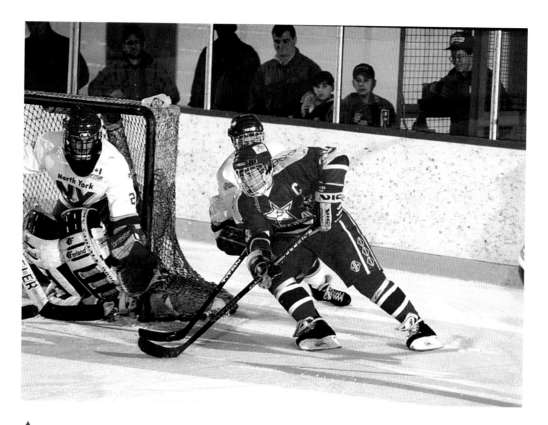

▲
Sergei Samsonov, one of the top prospects for the 1997 NHL Entry Draft, displayed his talents for North American scouts when the Moscow-based Central Red Army under–16 team embarked upon a rigorous 30-game exhibition tour in Ontario in December 1994 and January 1995.

▶

Jason Arnott, left, greets Edmonton Oilers' general manager Glen Sather after the Oilers made the Oshawa Generals product their number one pick — seventh overall — in the 1993 NHL Entry Draft.

▲◄
The "Kid Line" of Conacher, Primeau and Jackson in their prime during the glory days of the 1930s, above, and reunited as old-timers, at left. When Dick Irvin took over as coach of the Maple Leafs early in the 1931–32 season, he placed these three young stars together, and they captured the imagination of hockey fans everywhere. Charlie Conacher led the League in goals five times, won the scoring title twice and earned five consecutive All-Star berths. Busher Jackson, also a five-time All-Star, led the League in scoring in 1931–32. Joe Primeau, who went on win the Allan Cup, Memorial Cup and Stanley Cup as a coach, led the League in assists three times and won the Lady Byng Trophy in 1931–32.

▲
The much-feared "Production Line" of Gordie Howe, Sid Abel and Ted Lindsay as it appeared in 1950. The trio combined the leadership of Abel, the all-round skills of Howe and the feisty combativeness of Lindsay to lead the Red Wings to four first-place finishes and a pair of Stanley Cup championships.

▶
Almost two decades later, Detroit coach Bill Gadsby placed Frank Mahovlich on a line with Gordie Howe and Alex Delvecchio, forming one of the most potent trios to ever skate in the NHL. Mahovlich, Howe and Delvecchio combined for an NHL record 118 goals and amassed 264 points, a Detroit team record. Despite the success of the Wings' top forward unit and a 33–31–12 record, Detroit missed the playoffs in 1968–69

Broadcaster Wes McKnight, far left, and members of the
Boston Bruins famed "Kraut Line" — from left to right: Milt
Schmidt, Woody Dumart and Bobby Bauer — gather around
the microphone to talk hockey on the radio. The Krauts
propelled the Bruins to Stanley Cup titles in 1939 and 1941.
Each of the linemates was an NHL All-Star in 1940.

◄

From left to right: the unit of Bernie Geoffrion, Jean Beliveau and Bert Olmstead powered the Montreal Canadiens to a third consecutive Stanley Cup victory in 1956–57. Although both Geoffrion and Olmstead had mediocre regular seasons, they excelled in the playoffs. Olmstead led all post-season setup men with nine assists while Geoffrion and Beliveau finished first and second in playoff scoring.

▶

Propelled by the scoring exploits of the French Connection, the Buffalo Sabres emerged as one of the NHL elite teams in 1974–75, their fifth NHL season. The Sabres finished with 113 points and reached the Stanley Cup Finals. They were eliminated by Philadelphia in a championship series frequently delayed by fog rising from the ice surface in Buffalo's War Memorial Auditorium. Left winger Rick Martin, top, became the first player in the history of the franchise to record consecutive 50-goal seasons. He was selected fifth overall in the 1971 Amateur Draft and scored 44 goals as a rookie in 1971–72, setting an NHL record for first-year players that was eclipsed by Mike Bossy in 1977–78. Gilbert Perreault, center, was the franchise player around whom the Sabres' attack was built. The big center was the first player selected in the 1970 Amateur Draft, and won rookie of the year honors with 38 goals and 34 assists in 1970–71. He went on to become the first player drafted by the Sabres to earn induction into the Hockey Hall of Fame. He recorded two 100-point seasons for Buffalo and holds the franchise's career records for goals, assists and points. Right winger Rene Robert, bottom, played for both Toronto and Pittsburgh before joining the Sabres in 1971–72. He went on to score 20-or-more goals in each of his seven seasons in Buffalo. In 1974–75, he led the team in scoring with 40 goals and 60 assists. That season, the French Connection line combined for 291 points.

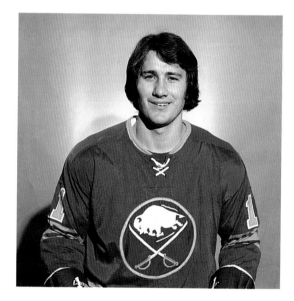

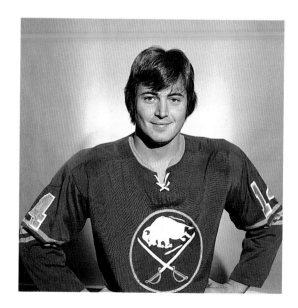

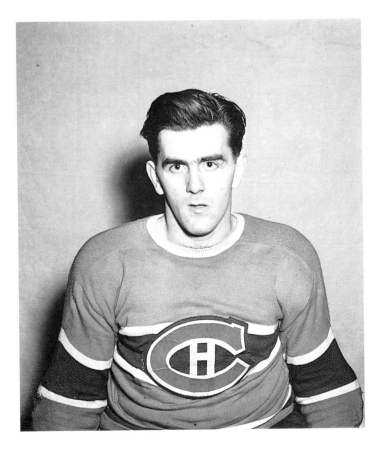

◄
After suffering season-ending leg injuries in his last year as a junior and his first season as a pro, many critics dismissed Maurice Richard as being too fragile to compete in the NHL. Perhaps that's why he played every game as though it might be his last. This intensity, evident even in this off-ice portrait, combined with his over-riding fear of losing, made the Rocket the most electrifying player to ever skate in the NHL.

▼
When the Rocket broke free from a defender and swept in alone on an opposing goaltender, his eyes were said to resemble glowing embers, searchlights or locomotive headlamps. Here, he burns Maple Leaf goaltender Turk Broda with a wicked wrist shot to the top corner during the 1945–46 season.

An almost serene Maurice Richard poses for one of hockey's earliest color portraits during the 1949–50 season. Even in repose, the Rocket still displays the intensity that made him the sport's premier big-game player.

Although Maurice Richard appears to have Harry Lumley at his mercy, the Rocket lost control of this puck at the last moment and it rolled harmlessly into the corner, preserving a 3–1 Toronto victory on December 11, 1954. Note the loose netting that hangs from the back of the old-style Art Ross goal frame.

Alex Delvecchio and Gordie Howe relax after a game during the 1960–61 season. As a teenager in Saskatoon, Howe was called the "slope-shouldered giant" because "everyone seemed smaller than me. Even if they were bigger, they just seemed smaller." In his first few seasons in the NHL, Howe proved that he could not only take the abuse thrown his way, he could dish it out as well, often so surreptitiously it went undetected by the on-ice officials.

This 1942 version of the King George Athletic Club bantam hockey team in Saskatoon, Saskatchewan included a youngster who would eventually be known as Mr. Hockey. Only five years after this photo was taken, Gordie Howe, top row, third from right, was a raw 18-year-old rookie with the Detroit Red Wings.

When this portrait of Howe was taken in 1954, he had just become the first player in NHL history to win four consecutive scoring titles.

Gordie Howe, who served as captain of the Red Wings from 1958–59 through 1961–62, uses his considerable strength to push Red Kelly off the puck during the 1960–61 season. Howe passed the captain's mantle to Alex Delvecchio prior to the start of 1962–63 campaign when Howe was named as the Red Wings playing-assistant coach.

◀ George "Chief" Armstrong, captain of the Toronto Maple Leafs, presents Gordie Howe with a gold puck commemorating Howe's 545th career goal prior to the Leafs–Red Wings tilt on November 30, 1963. Howe's 545th marker surpassed Maurice Richard's career total and gave Howe the NHL's all-time goal-scoring lead.

▶ In 1973, a 45-year-old Gordie Howe shocked the sporting world by coming out of retirement to join his sons Mark and Marty on the roster of the World Hockey Association's Houston Aeros. Four years and two 100-point seasons later, Gordie and his lads joined the New England Whalers, eventually following that team into the NHL when the League expanded in 1979.

◀ The hairline is receding and the face is fuller, but there is no mistaking the stride and the shoulders of Gordie Howe as he patrols the ice during an old timer's game that was part of the NHL's 1993 All-Star Weekend. A former teammate was once asked by a young sportswriter how many goals he thought Howe would score if were playing in the 1990s. When the graybeard answered "Oh, he'd be a 30-goal man easy," the rookie scribe remarked, "I thought he'd do better than that." At which point the old-timer slyly added "Of course, he'd be 67 years old if he were playing today."

Rookie rearguard Bobby Orr battles New York Ranger forward Phil Goyette for possession of a loose puck during the 1966–67 season. On November 26, 1966, only two weeks after this photo was taken, Orr suffered his first serious knee injury when he was checked into the boards by Toronto defenseman Marcel Pronovost. He returned to the lineup three weeks later, but was forced to undergo the first of many knee surgeries during the off-season.

Bobby Orr was only 14 years old when he first suited up for the Oshawa Generals in 1962–63. As Orr matured, both his offensive statistics and his defensive abilities improved. In 1965–66, his final year of junior, Orr collected 38 goals and 56 assists to finish third in scoring in the Ontario Junior Hockey League.

A sight many Boston Bruins fans believed they would never see: Orr in the uniform of the Chicago Black Hawks. Signed as a free agent by the Hawks in June 1976, Orr had already endured five knee operations when this photo was taken in March 1977. His sixth was only weeks away.

Bobby Orr's formidable arsenal of hockey skills was apparent from the moment he made his NHL debut with the Bruins. Heralded as a sure-fire superstar long before he arrived in Boston, Orr was a complete package even as a rookie. He possessed lightning acceleration, a big shot and whole-ice hockey vision. His ability to maneuver at top speed is apparent in this photo from his rookie campaign of 1966–67. Canadiens defenseman Jacques Laperriere (2), winner of the Norris Trophy in 1965–66, reacts as Orr wheels around in pursuit of a bouncing puck.

◀

The image of Bobby Orr leading an offensive rush and then turning on the jets to return to his own zone was a familiar sight throughout his remarkable career. Note the single band of tape on the blade of Orr's stick. Using almost no tape enabled Orr to better "feel" the puck on his stick. Throughout junior hockey, Orr used a fully taped stick, out of respect for his team's limited operating budget. He used a taped stick as an NHL rookie, but soon switched to the single-band technique. For many of the same reasons of "feel," Orr also wore no socks inside his skates.

◀

A youthful Orr and a pensive Jim Pappin do a slow waltz around the ice surface of Maple Leaf Gardens during Orr's first visit to Toronto as an NHLer on October 29, 1966.

▼

One of the major disappointments of Orr's career came in 1972 when a sore knee prohibited him from playing for Team Canada in its eight-game exhibition series against the Soviet National Team. Still, Orr was considered a member of the team, posed for team photos, participated in practices and traveled to Moscow with the club.

Wayne Gretzky, seen here during his first NHL season, had as many detractors as supporters when he joined the League in 1979–80 after a one-season sojourn in the World Hockey Association. Any doubt concerning the "Great One" and his talent was quickly dispelled when the 19-year-old became the youngest player in League history to score 50 goals in a season.

Sixteen NHL seasons later, Gretzky's achievements in the NHL literally fill a (record) book. He is a four-time Stanley Cup winner and has won the League's scoring championship ten times and its MVP award on nine occasions. No other player has scored 200 points in a season. Gretzky has accomplished this feat four times. He is the NHL's all-time regular-season and playoff leader in goals, assists and points. He has been the dominant player in the World Junior Tournament and the Canada Cup and has been the game's tireless ambassador, enhancing the NHL's profile in California, the rest of North America and throughout the hockey world.

Chicago Black Hawk coach Charlie Conacher, center, and his brother Roy, right, greet the newest Conacher to join the Black Hawk fold in October 1947. However, this newcomer, Jim Conacher, was no relation to the famous sporting family. Born in Motherwell, Scotland, where his father Robert was one of the country's best soccer players, Jim moved to Canada as a youngster and suited up with the Oshawa Generals, Omaha Knights, Indianapolis Capitols and Detroit Red Wings before joining the Black Hawks.

Worters   Connor   White   Burch.   Gorman.

"New York Americans" Runners up National Hoc

▼
"The Big Train," Lionel Conacher, stands to the right of manager
Red Dutton in this team photo of the 1928–29 New York
Americans. In addition to hockey, Conacher, who was named
Canada's male athlete of the half-century in 1950, excelled in
track and field, wrestling, boxing, lacrosse, baseball and football.
Like many teams of the era, the Amerks went on a barnstorming
tour after the conclusion of the season, stopping to pose for this
portrait in Portland, Oregon, on April 4, 1929. The original owner
of the Americans, Bill Dwyer, was a noted bootlegger which
probably explains the presence of the two bottles near the blade
of Rabbit McVeigh's stick at the far right.

This Montreal High School championship hockey team of 1899–1900 included the patriarch of hockey's royal family, Lester Patrick (front row, far left). Although Patrick grew up on Guy Street in Montreal, he spent a great deal of his sporting time in the affluent residential neighbourhood of Westmount. It was during this time that Patrick met Art Ross, another of hockey's great architects, eventually forging a friendship and rivalry that would last six decades.

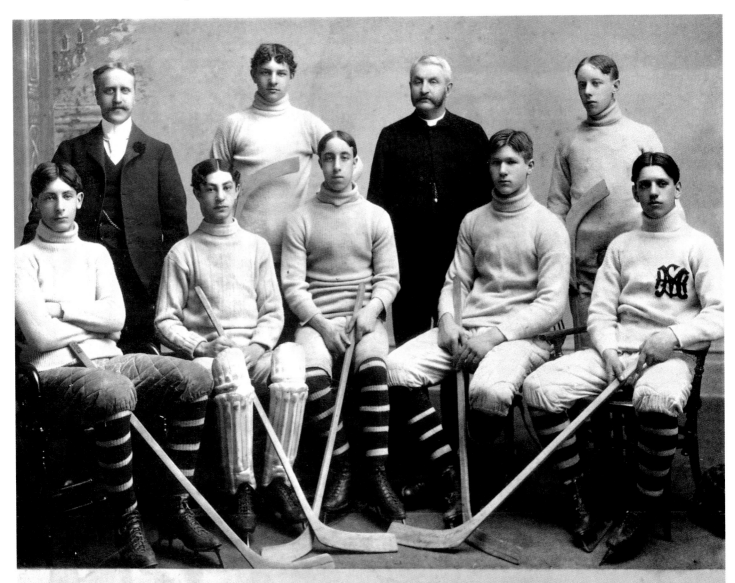

THE HIGH SCHOOL HOCKEY CLUB

~1899-1900~

WINNERS OF SENIOR CHAMPIONSHIP, INTER-SCHOOL HOCKEY LEAGUE.

W. B. T. MACAULAY, B.A., President H. S. A. A.	CONRAD HARRINGTON.	REV. ELSON I. REXFORD, B.A., Rector.	E. FOLEY.
LESTER PATRICK.	J. RUBIN.	PERCY FOLEY, Captain.	WALTER MOLSON.	HARRY LUCAS.

▶
New York Rangers' head coach and Hall-of-Fame forward Lynn Patrick explains a few defensive techniques to rookie blueliners Fred Shero, left, and Allan Stanley. Lynn, who guided the Rangers to the Stanley Cup Finals in 1950, was a son of Lester and brother of Muzz. He went on to have a long and productive career as a coach and general manager in the Boston Bruins and St. Louis Blues organizations. Both Stanley and Shero obviously learned from their mentor. On his way to the Hall of Fame as a defenseman, Stanley played on four Stanley Cup winners while Shero guided the Philadelphia Flyers to back-to-back championships in 1974 and 1975.

▼
Murray "Muzz" Patrick, right, is seen here with blueline partner Babe Pratt in 1939–40. He became the third member of the Patrick family to coach the Rangers when he took over behind the bench on January 6, 1954. The son of Lester Patrick, Muzz earned his coaching wings in St. Paul, Tacoma and Seattle before taking over on Broadway.

▼
When Craig Patrick had his name engraved on the Stanley Cup as the general manager of the Pittsburgh Penguins in 1991 and 1992, he became the third generation and fifth member of the Patrick clan to win hockey's most coveted prize. The son of Lynn and grandson of Lester, Craig played for five NHL teams before serving as a coach and general manager with the New York Rangers and Pittsburgh Penguins. He also managed the victorious U.S. Olympic Team in 1980.

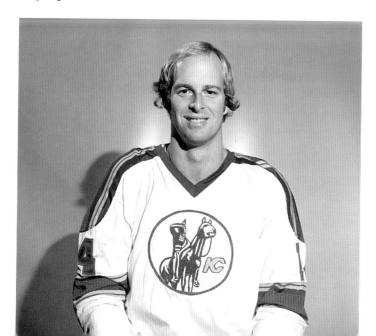

When Brett Hull, left, was named as the NHL's MVP in 1991, he joined his father Bobby Hull, right, in becoming the first father-son tandem to win the Hart Trophy. The Golden Jet won consecutive Hart Trophy awards in 1964–65 and 1965–66. While the "Golden Brett" and the "Golden Jet" may post similar statistical results, they display different techniques on the ice. Bobby Hull depended on speed, strength and a booming slapshot to pave his way to the Hall of Fame. Brett Hull's lightning-fast release, accurate wrist shot and ability to find open ice enabled him to reach the 50-goal plateau in five consecutive seasons with St. Louis.

◀

Irvine "Ace" Bailey, one of the Toronto Maple Leafs' first star attractions, was a durable right winger with a knack for finding the net. The NHL's scoring leader in 1928–29 when he recorded 22 goals and 32 points, Bailey had missed only 16 games in his career before suffering a near-fatal head injury on December 12, 1933, in Boston. The NHL's first All-Star Game was played as a benefit for Bailey and his family.

▼◀

Maple Leaf rookie Ron Ellis eyes the puck he fired past Boston's Eddie Johnston for his first NHL goal on October 17, 1964. Ellis' tally helped Toronto bounce the Bruins 7–2 for the Leafs' first home ice victory of the 1964–65 season.

▼

In addition to his skills as a diligent forechecker and penalty-killing specialist, Ron Ellis (seen here giving chase to Pittsburgh's Greg Polis during a 4–3 Toronto victory on February 17, 1971) was also a gifted offensive contributor, reaching the 20-goal plateau 11 times in his 16-year career with the Leafs.

Following Ace Bailey's injury and forced retirement, Toronto manager Conn Smythe decided that no other Maple Leaf player would ever wear Bailey's number six, effectively retiring that digit from active duty. Bailey stayed close to the game of hockey, and it was in his capacity as an off-ice official at Maple Leaf Gardens that he first spotted Ron Ellis, whose relentless work ethic reminded Bailey of himself. In 1968, Bailey requested that Ellis be permitted to don jersey number six and wear it for the duration of his career as a Leaf. On September 24, 1968, in a moving ceremony at the Gardens' Hot Stove Club, Ellis became the first Maple Leaf player in 34 years to wear Bailey's number.

Charlie Gardiner, the captain and inspirational leader of the Chicago Black Hawks poses in his All-Star uniform before the start of the Ace Bailey Benefit Game on February 14, 1934. Ironically, Gardiner's career was also cut short when the popular netminder suffered a brain hemorrhage only weeks after leading the Black Hawks to the Stanley Cup title in 1934. Although he was racked by severe headaches and pain throughout the regular season and playoffs, Gardiner still led all post-season goaltenders in wins (6), goals-against average (1.50) and shutouts (2).

Members of the 1934 All-Star Team that played the Leafs
in the Ace Bailey Benefit Game posed for this photo
shortly before donning their All-Star jerseys at Maple
Leaf Gardens. Top row, left to right: Charlie Gardiner,
Red Dutton, Eddie Shore, Allan Shields, unidentified,
Frank Finnigan, Lionel Conacher, Ching Johnson, Nels
Stewart. Front row, left to right: Normie Himes, Larry
Aurie, Hooley Smith, Jimmy Ward, Lester Patrick,
unidentified, Bill Cook, Howie Morenz, Aurel Joliat,
Herbie Lewis. Seated at front is mascot Howie Morenz, Jr.

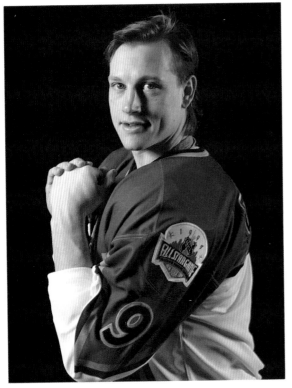

▲

Coach Tommy Ivan, second row, at far left, poses with the 1949 All-Star Team prior to taking the ice against the defending Stanley Cup champion Toronto Maple Leafs on October 10, 1949. The All-Stars received offensive support from Bob Goldham (front row, second from right), Paul Ronty (middle row, fifth from right) and Doug Bentley (back row, second from right) in a 3–1 victory over the Leafs in the NHL's third annual All-Star Game.

◄

Adam Graves, who collected a pair of assists in his first All-Star Game appearance during the 1994 mid-season classic in New York City, established a New York Ranger single-season record with 52 goals during the 1993–94 campaign. The modern NHL All-Star Game is played at mid-season and features two teams of All-Stars drawn from the League's Eastern and Western Conferences.

Superstars among the All-Stars, Gordie Howe and Bobby Hull share the spotlight prior to the NHL's 18th annual All-Star Game on October 10, 1964. The game marked Howe's 16th appearance in the pre-season classic and he played a key role in the All-Stars' 3–2 victory, assisting on Game MVP Jean Beliveau's goal midway through the second period.

During the 1940s, Bill Durnan, right, and Turk Broda, below, were the NHL's top netminders. Durnan won the Vezina Trophy six times while Broda played on three consecutive Stanley Cup winners. Both men went on to have successful minor-league coaching careers, but neither was given the opportunity to ply that trade in the NHL. Ironically, both men died within two weeks of each other in October 1972.

▼

Despite the best efforts of backchecking Toronto winger Howie Meeker, Dunc Fisher of the New York Rangers still manages to blast this wrist shot over the Broda's shoulder. Fisher's goal gave the Rangers a 1–0 lead over the Leafs, but Toronto stormed back with a pair of third period markers to register a 2–1 win on January 21, 1950.

▶

While he was still playing junior hockey in Toronto, Durnan learned to be ambidextrous by continuously switching his goal stick from hand to hand. When he finally decided to turn pro with the Montreal Canadiens in 1943, Durnan was equipped with special gloves that allowed him to catch with both hands and shoot from both sides. Durnan's unique style allowed him to always have his glove hand protecting the wide side of the net, confusing his opponents and helping him put the Vezina Trophy on his mantelpiece six times in his seven seasons in the NHL.

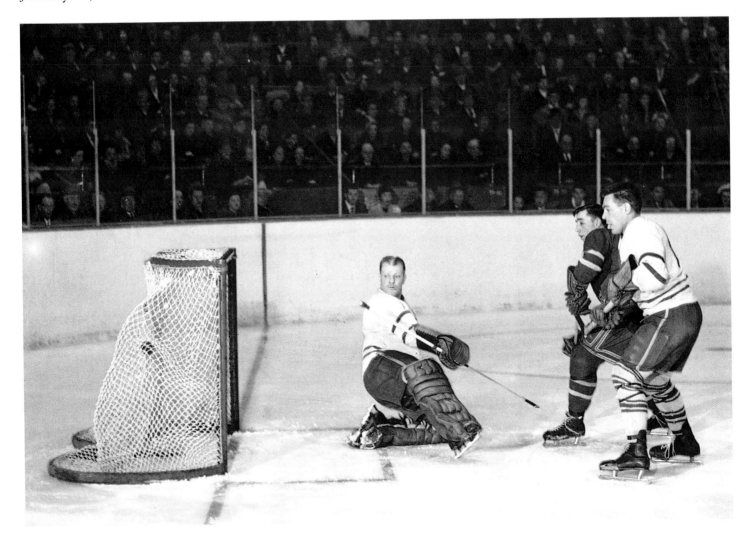

▶

The entire Montreal Canadiens' half of the ice surface opens up through the lens of the Turofsky Brothers camera. Toronto Maple Leaf coach Hap Day utilizes a rare offensive strategy by using four forwards on this Toronto powerplay. From left to right: Don Metz, Tod Sloan and Joe Klukay force the action around Montreal goaltender Bill Durnan while Max Bentley acts as the trailer. The Canadiens still managed to escape with a 4–1 victory.

▼

Gordie Howe, far right, buries one of his patented wrist shots behind Toronto goaltender Harry Lumley during the 1953–54 season. Although Howe's goal-scoring production dropped during this season, he still compiled a League-high 48 assists enabling him to win his fourth consecutive NHL scoring title.

◄
Throughout his career, Johnny Bower was considered to be the master of the pokecheck. Although he was best known for using this maneuver as a member of the Toronto Maple Leafs, his big goal stick would snake out when he was an NHL rookie with the New York Rangers in 1953–54. Here, he manages to deflect the puck away from an oncoming Rudy Migay during the Rangers' 5–2 win over Toronto on March 20, 1954.

◄
Maurice Richard blasts the 543rd goal of his career past Johnny Bower early in the second period of Montreal's 9–4 lopsided win over the Maple Leafs on March 9, 1960. The Rocket would only score two more goals in his career, a final regular-season marker and a final playoff goal, once again against Johnny Bower and the Leafs on April 12, 1960.

A young Jacques Plante, right, discusses defensive strategy with rookie Montreal coach Toe Blake during a mid-morning practice session during the 1955–56 season. With Blake as his coach, Plante would be selected to the NHL All-Star Team six times and would win the Vezina Trophy for fewest goals-against on six occasions. Together, the two would share in five consecutive Stanley Cup championships from 1956 to 1960.

The Gumper, Lorne "Gump" Worsley dives across the crease to rob the Toronto Maple Leafs of a scoring opportunity during this 4–4 tie on Saturday, December 13, 1958. Interested observers include, from left to right: Bill Gadsby, Bob Pulford, Les Colwill, John Hanna and Brian Cullen. The Leafs were the last NHL club of the six-team era to wear numbers on the sleeves of their jerseys, making the addition in 1961–62. Both teams have painted white numbers on their skate boots to aid newspaper photo editors with the task of player indentification. Note the CBC television camera behind the glass.

▶

Until the NHL required teams to dress two goaltenders in 1964, it was the responsibility of the home team to have a substitute goaltender available should the visiting team require his services. Just hours before the start of a March 9, 1959, game between Boston and Toronto, Bruin netminder Harry Lumley came down with the flu, forcing the Bruins to use a 20-year-old student goalie named Don Keenan. Seen here with Johnny Bower after the game, Keenan was a backup goalie at St. Michael's College in Toronto, but for one evening was the Bruins starting goaltender on national television. Keenan was very effective, allowing only four goals and earning a third-star selection. The following Monday it was back to the classroom for Keenan, who never played at the professional level again.

▼

This puck gets past Terry Sawchuk, but most didn't. The moody netminder from Winnipeg played in the NHL in four different decades, finishing with a record 103 shutouts and a lifetime goals-against average of 2.52. He posted a stunning goals-against average of 0.62 and four shutouts in the Red Wings eight-game Stanley Cup playoff sweep of 1952.

◄
Jacques Plante's rapier-like glove snags this shot off the stick of Toronto's Bob Pulford during the Maple Leafs 1–0 victory over Montreal on December 3, 1959. Plante, who had gone undefeated in 11 straight games since first putting on the mask, struggled through a six-game winless streak but refused to abandon his face protector.

▼
Even at the age of 41, Plante proves he still has excellent reflexes as he kicks away this shot from Los Angeles Kings forward Bob Berry (18). The mask Plante is wearing in this photo was his latest design, one that was to prove very popular among NHL, minor-pro and amateur goaltenders. By the early 1970s, Plante-designed masks were sold commercially.

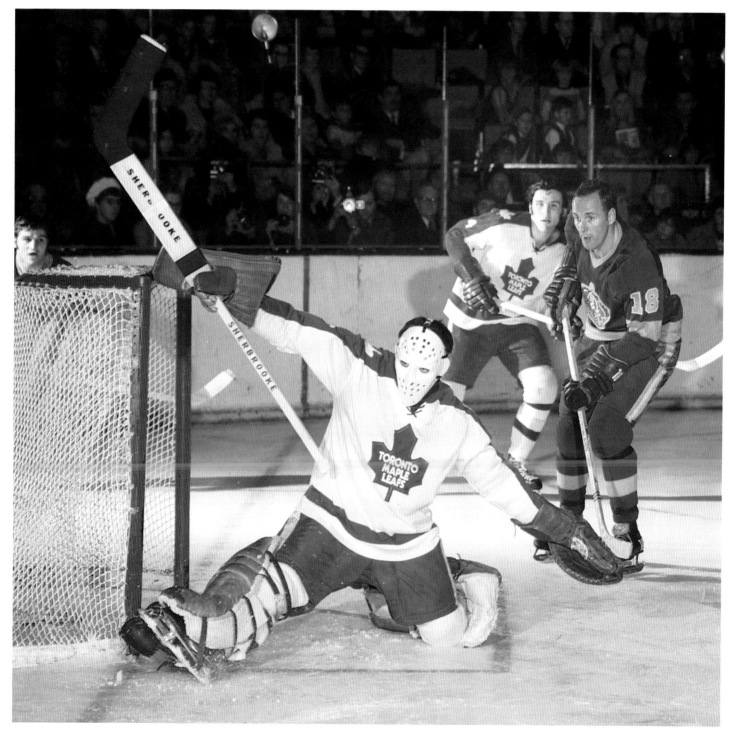

◀

After suffering countless facial injuries from sticks, skates and pucks, Terry Sawchuk became a convert to the mask during the 1962–63 season. He made his first appearance in Toronto wearing the mask on November 3 and led the Wings to a 7–3 trouncing of the defending Stanley Cup champions. Wearing the mask, Sawchuk won nine more games and lowered his goals-against average by nearly one goal during the season.

▼

Sawchuk, at center, is mobbed by his teammates after posting his 100th NHL shutout in a 3–0 victory over the Chicago Black Hawks on March 4, 1967. In Sawchuk's professional hockey career, including minor-league stops in Omaha and Indianapolis, he registered 113 shutouts. George Hainsworth, who recorded 10 shutouts with Saskatoon of the Western Hockey League and 94 zeros in the NHL, is the only other goaltender to reach the 100 shutout mark.

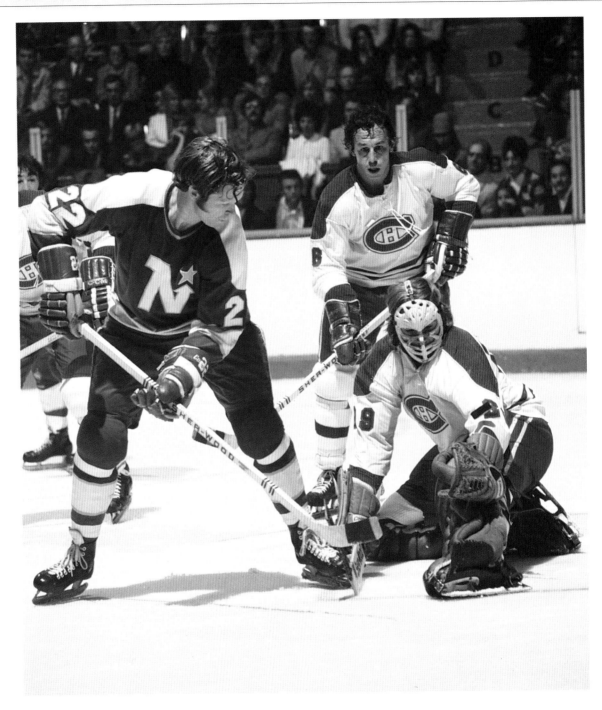

Minnesota's Dennis Hextall slips the puck over Ken Dryden's outstretched glove during the North Stars' 3–3 tie with the Canadiens on January 8, 1973. Dryden was the NHL's top netminder in 1972–73, leading all goaltenders with a 2.26 goals-against average.

Don Simmons became the second NHL goaltender to wear a mask when he took to the ice against the Toronto Maple Leafs on January 10, 1961. The mask wasn't an obstacle to Simmons, who shut out the Leafs by a score of 4–0.

▼
By the 1990s, most NHL goaltenders were wearing custom-fitted and decorated masks similar to the one modelled here by St. Louis' Curtis "Cujo" Joseph. His mask has a design that reflects his nickname, protection for the top and back of his head, shock-absorbing foam pads on the inside, an elongated chin to protect the lower face and neck and a wire "cage" that provides sight lines superior to those offered by all-fiberglass models.

▶
Eddy "The Eagle" Belfour's mask, complete with a screaming eagle, is similar to that worn by Curtis Joseph. Belfour's curved stick is visible in this photo, though he switched to a straighter blade in 1994–95.

▼
Dominik Hasek of the Buffalo Sabres wears a European-style "birdcage" mask that is a throwback to the type of mask he wore during his nine-year career in the Czechoslovakian National League.

◀

New York Rangers bench boss Frank Boucher, right, greets overtime hero Bryan Hextall in the visitor's dressing room after the Rangers' sixth-game victory over Toronto on April 9, 1940. The Rangers won back-to-back overtime games, including the Cup-clincher on Hextall's timely tally in game six. The 1940 championship was the Rangers third Stanley Cup title since the franchise joined the NHL in 1926–27.

◀ The Master's Voice. Foster Hewitt huddles in his gondola high above Maple Leaf Gardens, bringing the Maple Leafs into the living rooms of a million homes across Canada, Newfoundland and the United States. Working alone with only that evening's game program as his guide, Hewitt became the game's greatest ambassador and the most recognized voice in the history of the sport.

▶ Although they were often a poor outfit on the ice, the New York Americans traveled in style during the 1939–40 playoffs. During their best-of-three set with the Detroit Red Wings, the Amerks took to the friendly skies with United Air Lines as they journeyed from city to city.

◀ It's not often that NHL teams take to sea to ply their trade, but after the 1937–38 campaign, the Detroit Red Wings climbed aboard an ocean liner and sailed to Europe for a series of exhibition games against the Montreal Canadiens.

▶ Future Hall-of-Famers Bill Cowley, left, and Dit Clapper examine the puck from a game-winning playoff goal. Cowley led all post-season scorers in the 1939 playoffs with 11 assists and 14 points in 12 games for the Bruins. His best years were still to come. He went on to win the Hart Trophy on two occasions and the Art Ross once during the early 1940s. Clapper, who earned NHL All-Star recognition as both a forward and a defenseman, went on to become the League's first 20-year veteran. Clapper also coached the Bruins from 1945–46 to 1948–49.

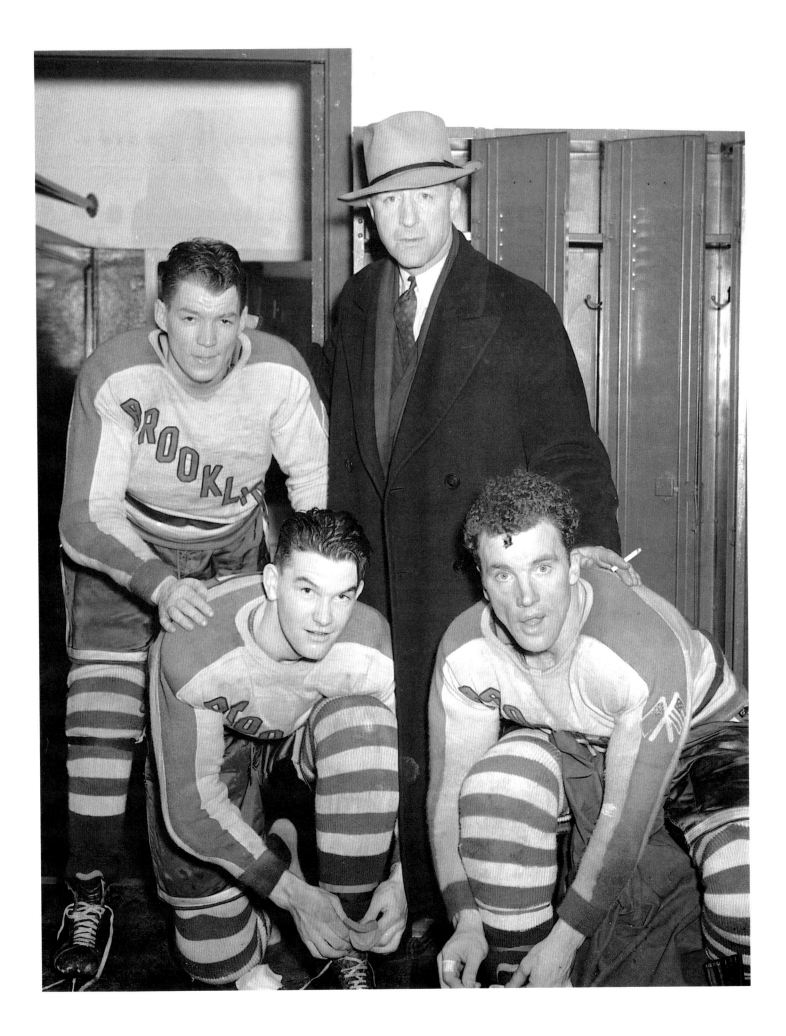

Prior to the 1941–42 season, the struggling New York Americans franchise was renamed the Brooklyn Americans, although the team continued to play out of Madison Square Garden. With coach Red Dutton are, from left to right, Wilf Field, Harry "Whipper" Watson and "Boxcar" Pat Egan during the Amerks' last season. Watson and teammate Ken Mosdell were the last two members of the Brooklyn team to retire from pro hockey. Watson finished his playing career after one final season with the Buffalo Bisons of the AHL in 1958–59, while Mosdell played until 1959–60 with the Montreal Royals of the Quebec Hockey League.

Bryan Hextall (12) welcomes former Chicago Black Hawk defenseman Joe Cooper back into the New York Rangers fold during the 1946-47 campaign. Cooper, who began his career with New York in 1935-36 before joining the Hawks in 1938, returned to the Rangers in 1946 to replace Ott Heller who had retired at the end of the 1945-46 season.

Steve Wojciechowski suits up in the Detroit Red Wings dressing room during the 1944–45 season. Note the exposed elbow pads and the patch on his shoulder, imploring everybody to buy "at least 10% in war bonds." Wojciechowski, who had the longest last name of any player in NHL history, was known simply as "Wochy" during his brief tour of duty in the NHL.

Chicago's Tod "Slinker" Sloan poses in the dressing room after ripping a pair of pucks past former teammate Johnny Bower during the 1960–61 season. Sloan and Ted Lindsay were both banished to the lowly Black Hawks prior to the 1958–59 season because of their work in attempting to organize an NHL players' association.

Even in the dressing room after a game, Maurice Richard, left, often retained his intense demeanor. In contrast, his linemate Toe Blake possessed the ability to leave the game on the ice. Blake's even keel would later make him the perfect candidate to coach the Montreal Canadiens and harness the Rocket's considerable fury.

Each of these four Toronto Maple Leaf skaters played a winning hand in the Leafs' 4–2 victory over Montreal in game three of the 1947 Stanley Cup finals. From left to right: Vic Lynn, Gus Mortson, Ted Kennedy and Bud Poile each scored a goal as the Leafs took a 2–1 lead in the best-of-seven championship final.

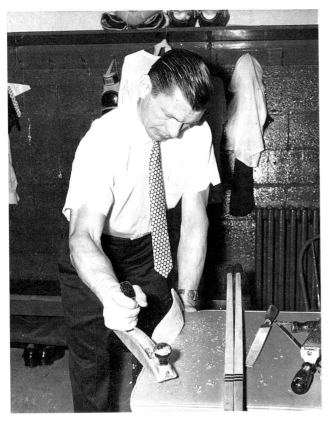

◀

The atmosphere in a dressing room leading up to a hockey game is one of calculated preparation. Every player readies himself in his own special way. For Chicago Black Hawks center Stan Mikita in October of 1967 that meant putting his carpentry skills to good use and carefully planing down the "banana-blade" of his hockey stick.

▼

During the NHL's first 50 seasons, riding the rails was the standard mode of transportation. It wasn't uncommon for both teams, the media and even fans to travel together on the train. Here, a porter greets Toronto Maple Leaf stars (left to right) Johnny Bower, Frank Mahovlich, Allan Stanley and Ron Stewart as the Leafs board for an overnight trip to Boston.

During the 1958–59 season, newly appointed Maple Leafs coach Punch Imlach predicted that Toronto would overtake the New York Rangers and advance to the Stanley Cup playoffs. On hearing of Imlach's prophesy, Rangers' coach Phil Watson remarked, "The only crystal ball he's got is on his shoulders. What a beautiful head of skin." However, when these half-dozen Leaf players — including Brian Cullen, Bob Pulford and Dick Duff — joined swami King Clancy to peer into Imlach's "crystal ball," they saw the bald prognosticator's elaborate plans for a Maple Leaf dynasty that would bring four Stanley Cup titles to Toronto in the 1960s.

▼
A quartet of happy Habs — from left to right: Henri Richard, Jean Beliveau, John Ferguson and Yvan Cournoyer — celebrates in the Canadiens dressing room after Montreal downed the defending Stanley Cup champion Toronto Maple Leafs four games to two in the 1965 semi-finals. The Canadiens battled back from a 3–1 first period deficit in the sixth match to win on Claude Provost's goal at 16:33 of the first overtime period.

▶
A reflective Bobby Baun relaxes with the toast of champions after the Toronto Maple Leafs' exciting seven-game victory over Detroit in the 1964 Stanley Cup finals. Baun played the seventh game with a fractured ankle, an injury he sustained shortly before scoring the game-winning overtime goal in game six.

The Montreal Shamrocks, who defeated the defending
Stanley Cup champion Montreal Victorias 1–0 to assure
themselves of a first-place finish in the Canadian Amateur
Hockey League, pose with the original Stanley Cup bowl. As
specified in the rules governing the Stanley Cup, the Victorias
passed the championship trophy to the Shamrocks. On
March 14, 1899, the Shamrocks successfully defended their
crown with a 6–2 victory over Queen's University. The 1899
team included future Hall-of-Fame members Fred Scanlan
(seated second from left), Harry Trihey (seated third from left)
and Art Farrell (standing, far right). Farrell was also well-
known for writing hockey's first history and rule book.

This powerhouse Quebec Bulldogs team featured the goaltending of Paddy Moran, the aggressiveness of "Bad" Joe Hall, the finesse of Joe Malone and the firepower of Jack McDonald. Joe Malone's goal at 23:50 of overtime on March 3, 1913, gave the Bulldogs a 6–5 win over Ottawa to win both the National Hockey Association title and the Stanley Cup. The 'Dogs then buried the Moncton Hawks 9–3 and 8–0 to retain the trophy. Note that the Cup already has a pair of extra collars attached to its base.

Toronto Maple Leafs coach Hap Day poses with a rapidly growing Stanley Cup after the 1942 Leafs became the only team in sports history to win a best-of-seven championship final after trailing three games to none. As part of the victory celebration, Day decided to don the Leaf uniform and pose with the fruits of that incredible victory, the Stanley Cup.

Standing under a montage of magical Maple Leaf moments, a pair of champions pose with the spoils of victory in April 1947. Joe Primeau, right, coach of St. Michael's College in Toronto, caresses the Memorial Cup, symbolic of the Canada's junior hockey championship. Maple Leafs general manager Conn Smythe, left, clutches the "bird-bath" Stanley Cup after Toronto downed the Montreal Canadiens in six games. This elongated version of the Cup was introduced in 1941, and the Leafs' victory in 1947 marked the third time the club had enjoyed this very special "silver cigar."

In a rare show of affection for the opposition, "Terrible" Ted Lindsay, right, congratulates Toronto's Gus Mortson following the Maple Leafs four-game sweep of the Red Wings in the 1949 Stanley Cup Finals. Mortson and Lindsay were teammates with the St. Michael's College Majors and were added to Oshawa's Memorial Cup-winning squad in 1943–44. (See photo on page 64.)

Detroit goaltender Harry Lumley searches for a rebound between a maze of skates and sticks as Red Wing defender Leo Reise attempts to clear New York Ranger right winger Jack McLean out the crease area during action in game two of the 1950 Stanley Cup Finals. Forced to play the entire series on the road because the circus was making its annual pilgrimage to Madison Square Garden, the Rangers opted to play games two and three in Toronto. New York held on to defeat Detroit 3–1 in this game on a pair of third-period goals by Edgar Laprade.

Bill Barilko's Stanley Cup-winning goal in the 1951 Finals remains one of the most famous images in Stanley Cup history. Barilko, a hard-hitting defenseman whose exuberance sometimes outshone his talent, had been warned by Leaf coach Joe Primeau not to wander into the offensive zone. However, at 2:53 in overtime in game five, he surged in from the blueline and back-handed a loose puck over a sprawling Gerry McNeil in the Montreal net. The other on-ice witnesses to Barilko's mastery were, left to right, Maurice Richard, Howie Meeker, Tom Johnson, referee Bill Chadwick, Cal Gardner and Butch Bouchard.

In 1948, the Stanley Cup changed shape again, moving from the lengthy "cigar-shaped" model to a barrel-like two-piece trophy. The new design dictated that when the trophy was presented after each season's final playoff game, the team captain would lift the top half and leave the barrel on a sturdy table that had been brought out onto the ice. On April 16, 1949, newly appointed Leaf captain Ted Kennedy joined NHL president Clarence Campbell and his teammates on the ice at Maple Leaf Gardens to savour Toronto's third consecutive Stanley Cup title.

The Canadiens won an unprecedented fifth consecutive Stanley Cup in 1960. In this vaguely disquieting image from that year's Finals, a vulnerable-looking Jacques Plante peers at the play developing in front of him, hoping for a moment's respite to dart out and recover his stick. Plante's apparent vulnerability is just a trick of the Turofsky camera: in 1960, the Canadiens won eight straight playoff games and allowed only five goals against in the Finals. Plante's mask is his second design, a well-ventilated web-like fiberglass model that fit close to the face. Plante wore this design until 1965, and many other goaltenders who adopted face protection wore similar styles.

▼

Three backchecking Maple Leaf forwards, left to right, George Armstrong, Gerry Ehman and Red Kelly, look on in disbelief as Johnny Bower, the venerable China Wall, snags a hot shot off the stick of Gordie Howe during the opening game of the 1964 Stanley Cup Finals. Although Howe later solved Bower for a goal, Bob Pulford's breakaway winner with only two seconds left in the game gave the Maple Leafs a 3–2 victory over the determined Detroit side.

▶

In a shining example of Stanley Cup shinny, six members of the Montreal Canadiens and Detroit Red Wings battle for possession of a loose puck during game one of the 1966 Stanley Cup Finals. The on-ice combatants are, from left to right, Dick Duff, Norm Ullman, Leo Boivin, Henri Richard, Bobby Rousseau and Bill Gadsby.

◀

The 1969–70 Boston Bruins pose with the Stanley Cup shortly after Bobby Orr's dramatic overtime goal in game four of the finals gave the Bruins their first championship in 29 years. The trophy itself underwent a major overhaul in the 1950s and 1960s. The variegated bands that made up the barrel of the trophy were removed and replaced by bands of equal width. The resulting one-piece trophy has retained the same size and shape ever since. The original bowl, brittle after almost 80 years of wear and tear, was retired to the Hockey Hall of Fame and replaced with an exact replica.

◀

Former two-time Art Ross Trophy winner Dickie Moore (12) begins an offensive rush under the watchful gaze of goaltender Glenn Hall and Montreal defender Serge Savard (18) during game four of the 1968 Finals. Moore ended a two-year retirement to join the expansion St. Louis Blues midway through the 1967–68 season. Hall won the Conn Smythe Trophy as playoff MVP, while Moore contributed 14 playoff points — the second highest total of his career.

▼

Bob Nystrom redirects the puck past Philadelphia Flyer goaltender Pete Peeters at the 7:11 mark of the first overtime period to give the New York Islanders a 5–4 victory and deliver the club's first Stanley Cup title to the fans at Nassau Coliseum on May 24, 1980. Nystrom, one of only four Islander players to have his number retired, scored four career overtime goals, tying him for second place in the all-time playoff record book. This photo was taken by an Islanders fan with an exquisite sense of timing.

◄

Craig MacTavish of the New York Rangers finds himself surrounded by a trio of Vancouver defenders — Brian Glynn (28), Kirk McLean (1) and Pavel Bure (10) — during game six of the 1994 Stanley Cup Finals. MacTavish, the last player in the NHL to play without a helmet, earned his fourth Stanley Cup ring when the Rangers outlasted the Canucks in a marathon seven-game series. The win was the Rangers' first Cup championship since 1940.

▼

The pose that refreshes. Scott Stevens, captain of the New Jersey Devils, fulfills the dream of almost every young hockey player by hoisting the Stanley Cup in front of an adoring home crowd at the Brendan Byrne Meadowlands Arena on June 24, 1995. The Devils, who had come within an overtime goal of reaching the Stanley Cup Finals in 1994, ensured that their names would be engraved on the trophy for 1995 by eliminating the Detroit Red Wings in four straight games.

My Three Sons. Toronto defenseman Bobby Baun and his wife Sally show off the Stanley Cup to their brood after the Leafs defeated the Detroit Red Wings in the 1963 Stanley Cup Finals.

◀

Thank Heaven for Little Girls. Tim and Lori Horton are surrounded by their four fashionable daughters after the Maple Leafs captured the Stanley Cup in May 1967.

▼

Don't Mess with the Messiers. The Messier family gathers with the fruits of Mark's labors — the Stanley Cup, the Hart Trophy and a mini Hart Trophy replica — following "A Celebration of Excellence, " the NHL's end-of-season awards gala for 1989–90.

◄
Fans and newspaper reporters in the Montreal media howled when the Canadiens traded local hero Newsy Lalonde to Saskatoon for an unknown commodity named Aurel Joliat in 1922. Two seasons later, with the Stanley Cup tucked safely under his arm, Joliat was welcomed as a conquering hero after the Canadiens downed the Vancouver Maroons and Calgary Tigers to win the Stanley Cup title.

▶
Although he was popularly dubbed the Stratford Streak and the Mitchell Meteor in the press, Howie Morenz could best be described as the "Babe Ruth of Hockey." Morenz's presence in the Montreal Canadiens lineup kept fans in the seats and dollars in the till around the NHL during the early years of the Depression.

SECTION TWO

THE

GAME

◀

One of the first natives of Ontario's Lakehead region to star in the NHL, Tommy Cook played nine seasons with Chicago and the Montreal Maroons. An original member of the "Thundering Herd," the Fort William senior team that lost to the Varsity Blues in the 1927 Allan Cup finals in Vancouver, Cook spent eight seasons with the Chicago Black Hawks and led the team in scoring twice before being traded to the Montreal Maroons for Carl Voss in 1937.

▼

Four former members of the Toronto Maple Leafs, left to right: Charlie Conacher, Buzz Boll, Murray Armstrong and Busher Jackson, meet again at Maple Leaf Gardens after joining the New York Americans in the 1939–40 season. The Americans became known as the NHL's "All-Star Retirement Home" because so many future Hall-of-Famers, such as Conacher, Jackson, Nels Stewart, Eddie Shore, Hap Day and Roy Worters played with the team late in their NHL careers.

▲

A beaming "Bonnie Prince Charlie" Rayner receives a poppy during the Remembrance Day campaign in November 1946. After four last-place finishes in a row, the Rangers attempted to change their luck with new uniforms, adopting a jersey with the number on the front. While the alteration may have helped Rayner lead the League with five shutouts, the Blueshirts missed the playoffs once again. The next year the old-style jersey with the word Rangers printed diagonally across the chest returned, and the team made the playoffs for the first time since 1942.

▶

When he made his NHL debut early in the 1942–43 season, Armand "Bep" Guidolin was 16 years old, making him the youngest player to ever skate in the League. When Boston manager Art Ross placed "The Bepper" on a line with fellow teenagers Don Gallinger and Bill Shill, the trio became known as the "Sprout Line." Unlike baseball's Joe Nuxhall, who also made his major-league debut at age 16, Guidolin proved he could play with the big boys, spending nine seasons in the NHL with Boston, Detroit and Chicago.

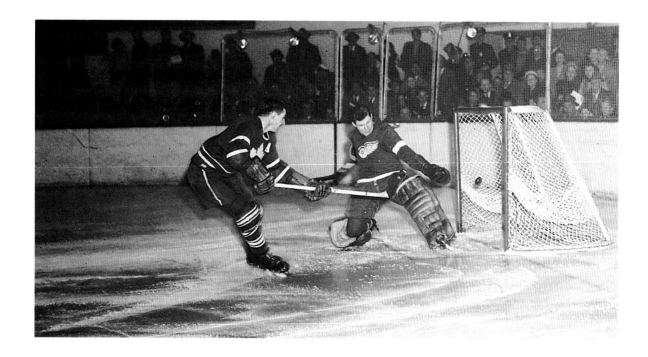

◀

Milestone, Saskatchewan, native Garth Boesch was instantly recognizable during his four-year career because he was the only player in the NHL to wear a mustache. Boesch joined the Toronto Maple Leafs in 1946–47 after three years playing senior hockey with the RCAF in Saskatoon and one season with the AHL's Pittsburgh Hornets. Four seasons and three Stanley Cup titles later, his father's death prompted Boesch to return to the family farm and "make some real money."

▲

Max Bentley flips a wrist shot past the unfolding glove of Detroit goaltender Harry Lumley during game one of the 1949 Stanley Cup Finals at Detroit's Olympia. Although the Red Wings opened the scoring in three games, the Maple Leafs swept the Wings out of Stanley Cup competition with four consecutive wins.

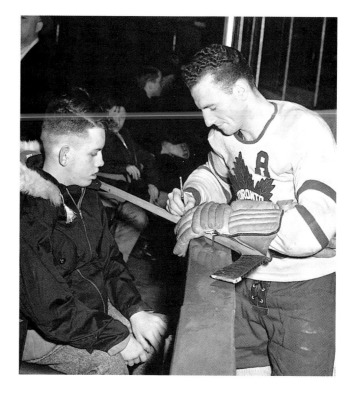

▶

Before the introduction of glass protection along the side boards, rail seats afforded fans the opportunity to see the action up close and ask for the occasional autograph. A young Ted Kennedy obliges this fan during the 1947–48 season, a year before "Teeder" assumed the captaincy of the Maple Leafs.

A proud Ted Kennedy embraces the collars and barrel of the Stanley Cup after Bill Barilko's overtime goal gave the Toronto Maple Leafs a 3–2 victory over the Montreal Canadiens in the fifth and deciding game of the 1951 championship finals. At this time, the Cup was still a two-piece trophy that split where the collars met the barrel.

Johnny Crawford of the Boston Bruins was famous for wearing a helmet, partly for protection but mostly to hide his bald head. Here, he wards off the forechecking of Don Metz during the Bruins' 25th anniversary season of 1948–49. The "hubbed B" on Crawford's uniform was introduced to mark the anniversary and featured the numbers 24 and 49 embroidered on either side of the "B." Fans in Boston, which is known as the Hub City, liked the new style and it eventually became the Bruins' standard attire.

◄

Cal Gardner (17) slips the puck past Harry Lumley's outstretched pad as Chicago defender Lee Fogolin tries in vain to reach the speedy Leaf forward during Toronto's 3–0 victory over the Black Hawks on March 3, 1951.

◄▼

During the 1950s, the Chicago Black Hawks franchise was in trouble, both on the ice and at the box office. To bolster the Hawks, the NHL Board of Governors created a "have and have-not" program that provided support for struggling teams in the form of players and/or cash. During the 1952–53 season, these three former Maple Leafs (left to right: Vic Lynn, Al Rollins and Gus Mortson) found themselves reunited as members of the Black Hawks.

▼

Boston's Bill Quackenbush (11) appears to trip up Ron Stewart as the Maple Leaf right winger attempts to track down a rebound during this meeting between the Bruins and Leafs in 1954–55. Boston captain Milt Schmidt, seen here giving Bruin netminder "Sugar" Jim Henry a helping hand, retired shortly after this photo was taken to become the eighth coach of the Boston Bruins.

Professional hockey's true "ironman" Andy Hebenton played 1,062 consecutive games in the Western Hockey League and the NHL until finally missing a contest during the 1967–68 season. Hebenton's streak, which began in 1951–52 when he was wearing the jersey of the WHL's Victoria Cougars, continued through his NHL employment in New York and Boston to his return to the WHL with Portland and Victoria. In the end, it wasn't bumps, bangs, bruises or breaks that kept Hebenton out of the lineup. On October 18, 1967, Andy Hebenton attended his father's funeral and missed his first game since March 8, 1952.

The American Hockey League's rookie-of-the-year in 1951–52 and the Western Hockey League's leading scorer in 1952–53, Earl "Dutch" Reibel enjoyed a successful six-year career in the NHL. He set an NHL record for most assists by a player in his first NHL game with four on October 8, 1953, was a member of two Stanley Cup-winning teams in Detroit and was the Lady Byng Trophy winner in 1955–56. After NHL tours in Chicago and Boston, he finished his professional career with the AHL's Providence Reds.

◄▲
During his 24-year career as an NHL defenseman, Tim Horton was adept at cutting off the skating lanes and keeping opposition forwards to the outside. In this photo from the 1956–57 season, he intercepts New York Ranger center Red Sullivan and escorts him into the boards.

◄

This herd of happy Habs practice their post-game victory leap, a necessary procedure given that the Canadiens won 242 regular season and playoff games from 1955–56 to 1959–60. Joining in on the success salute are, from left to right, Marcel Bonin, Bernie Geoffrion, Phil Goyette, Henri Richard, Dickie Moore and Jean Beliveau.

▲
An unmasked Terry Sawchuk glances back to see Bob Pulford's shot bulging the twine during this Toronto-Detroit matchup midway through the 1960–61 season. Gordie Howe (9) and Marcel Pronovost (3) are the defending Red Wings who have just had their pockets picked by the pesky Pulford. Careful examination of the ad-free boards in this photo reveals that they are made of individual planks and have a white "kickplate" at the bottom. Just visible at the top right are double doors that swung outward onto the ice. League rules would soon require a colored kickplate and doors that swung inward.

▼

Vic Stasiuk (7) has Johnny Bower down and at his mercy despite the best efforts of Bob Pulford and Brian Cullen during this spirited Toronto-Boston matchup during the 1958–59 season. Though this photograph was shot with black-and-white film, it's apparent that both the Leafs and the Bruins are wearing colored gloves, replacing the beige or brown leather gauntlets that had been the standard in the NHL for almost 40 years.

▶

Stasiuk, seen here making a bold fashion statement during the 1959–60 season, was one of the trigger-man on the Boston Bruins' famous "Uke Line." He had his name engraved on the Stanley Cup three times as a member of the Detroit Red Wings before joining the Bruins in 1955–56 where he was teamed with Bronco Horvath and John Bucyk, two other players of Ukrainian descent. As a member of the Ukes, Stasiuk had the most productive seasons of his career and reached the Stanley Cup Finals in 1957 and 1958. He scored a career-high 29 goals and 68 points in 1959–60.

◄
A worried looking Frank Mahovlich puts the grab on Montreal's Jean-Guy Talbot during the 1960–61 season, Mahovlich's finest campaign as a Leaf.

▶

On November 1, 1959, ironically just one day after Halloween, Jacques Plante became the first goaltender to wear a full face mask in an NHL game. Three weeks later, on November 21, fans at Maple Leaf Gardens got their first opportunity to see the masked marvel when the Montreal Canadiens downed the Leafs 4–1. Plante designed and built this first mask, and though it did little more than protect his face from cuts, he continued to wear it until the playoffs, when he introduced a new and improved model.

▼

Photographers' strobe lights cast an eerie glow across the ice surface at Maple Leaf Gardens as the Toronto Maple Leafs and Chicago Black Hawks battle during the 1960–61 season. The players in this drama include, left to right, Reg Fleming, Elmer Vasko, Billy Harris, Frank Mahovlich, Pierre Pilote, Glenn Hall and Bob Nevin.

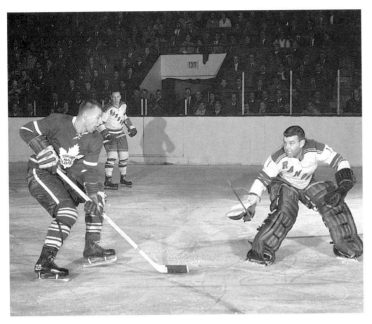

▲

Although Gump Worsley appears to be taking up an "*en garde*" stance against an onrushing Eddie Shack, he has just swept a loose puck away from the front of the New York Rangers' crease.

▼

Hockey fans sat poised on the edges of their seats throughout the 1960–61 season as two players – Frank Mahovlich and Bernie Geoffrion – roared down the stretch with a chance to reach the 50-goal plateau. On March 4, 1961, Mahovlich nestled this low drive just inside the post to give him 47 goals for the season. The "Big M" could score only one more goal in his final six games, allowing Geoffrion to pass him and become only the second player in NHL history to score 50 goals in a season.

Harry Howell, who played 24 seasons in the NHL and World Hockey Association without ever appearing on a championship team, finally had his name engraved on the Stanley Cup as a scout with the 1990 Edmonton Oilers.

◀

Willie O'Ree, the first black athlete to play in the NHL, carried the torch of racial equality first lit by minor-league stars like Art Dorrington, Herb and Ozzie Carnegie and Manny McIntyre throughout the 1960s and 1970s. Although O'Ree's stay in the NHL was brief — he appeared in only 45 games with the Boston Bruins from 1957–58 to 1960–61 — he continued to play professional hockey until the Western Hockey League suspended operations in 1974.

▼

Boston forward Wayne Hicks (12) upends Bob Pulford (20), but not before the crafty Maple Leaf winger slips the puck past Bruins' netminder "Miche" Perreault to give Toronto a 5–1 lead on December 1, 1962. Perreault, who had seen his first NHL action with the Montreal Canadiens in 1955–56, joined the Bruins for the 1962–63 season, appearing in 22 games. Eleven seasons later, he re-surfaced in the WHA and was one of only three goaltenders to play without a face mask in the rival pro loop.

Veteran Toronto Maple Leaf defenseman Allan Stanley dives in an attempt to knock the puck away from Gordie Howe early in the first period of the 17th annual NHL All-Star Game on October 5, 1963. Stanley was sent to the penalty box moments later, and Howe wasted little time in setting up Henri Richard, whose powerplay goal at 4:08 of the frame pulled the All-Stars into a 1–1 tie. Every year the All-Stars would play the Stanley Cup champions in a pre-season encounter until 1966–67 when the game was shifted to a mid-season date. The All-Stars-vs.-Cup-champion format was replaced by a game between All-Stars from the League's East and West divisions in 1969.

◄

Jean Beliveau's leadership, dignity and discipline both on and off the ice made him a cultural icon in Quebec and a respected athlete throughout the sporting world. More than twenty years after he retired as a player, Beliveau is still held in such high regard that in 1994 he was offered the opportunity to serve as Canada's Governor-General. Citing a desire to spend more time with his family, Beliveau declined with many thanks.

▼

Norm Ullman (7) breaks away from Andy Bathgate (9) with linemate Floyd Smith (17) in tow and slams a shot past Leaf goaltender Terry Sawchuk to help Detroit down Toronto 4–2 on March 10, 1965. Ullman went on to lead the NHL with 42 goals, joining Bernie Geoffrion as the only players not named Howe or Hull to lead the League in "lighting the lamp" in the 1960s.

Although he had been in the Montreal Canadiens' system since 1952, Charlie Hodge was never considered a prime candidate to be the club's number-one goaltender. When he was handed the job prior to the 1963–64 season, Hodge responded by winning the Vezina Trophy with a goals-against average of 2.26. Thanks to sprawling saves like this one against Bob Pulford, Hodge also registered a League-leading eight shutouts.

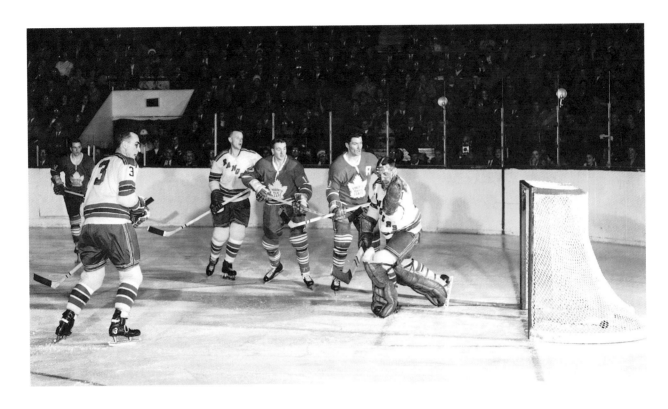

The craft of the backhand shot became a lost art in the 1960s when the curved stick became the weapon of choice for many NHL players. Dave Keon, however, played much of his career with little or no curve in his stick. Here, he eludes New York defenders Rod Seiling (16) and Vic Hadfield (11) only to be robbed by Eddie Giacomin during Toronto's 5–2 win over the Rangers on November 13, 1965.

◄

On March 14, 1964, the New York Rangers made their first visit to Maple Leaf Gardens since the blockbuster trade that sent Andy Bathgate and Don McKenney to the Leafs for five Toronto players. Only 3:13 into the game, Dave Keon, far left, sent a shot toward the Rangers net that eluded goaltender Jacques Plante and defenders Harry Howell (3) and Ron Ingram (4). Both McKenney (17) and Bathgate (9) picked up assists on the goal as the Leafs went on to post a 7–3 victory.

▼

Unlike many photographers of the day, Frank Prazak often positioned his lens above the glass and shot down on the action, enabling him to close in on his subjects. In this image from the 1964–65 season, Toronto's Red Kelly wards off Detroit's Pit Martin in an attempt to clear the puck out of the Maple Leafs zone. By the mid-1960s, Kelly was one of a handful of players to wear a helmet.

The stylish acrobatics of Detroit goaltender Roger Crozier fascinated fans during the 1965–66 season. Although Crozier's rapier-like leg saves captured the on-ice attention of Doug Barkley and Frank Mahovlich, the Leafs managed to slip four pucks past him in a 4–3 Toronto victory on October 30, 1965.

The camera isolates Detroit's Paul Henderson and New York Ranger defenseman Rod Seiling so that they appear to have the entire ice surface to themselves. The straight sticks, no helmets, ad-free boards, low protective glass and suits and ties in the crowd speak of another era.

▼
Rod Gilbert uses the cross-over step to accelerate around Maple Leaf defenseman Al Arbour during the 1965–66 season. Note the goal judge with the NHL crest on his coat pocket sitting amidst the fans in Madison Square Garden. Although the NHL would soon require the goal judge to be separated from the crowd by some sort of enclosure, not every arena fulfilled that obligation. Today, Maple Leaf Gardens still has open goal judge areas.

▶
Nothing adds to a hockey photo like the presence of the puck in flight. Here, Montreal goaltender Charlie Hodge throws out a pad and deflects the puck toward the corner with the ever-dangerous Black Hawk sharpshooter Stan Mikita standing on the edge of the crease.

▼
The fight for position in the offensive zone between an attacking forward and a back-checking defenseman frequently results in a fierce struggle for territory. Often, as in the battle pictured here between Rangers policeman Reggie Fleming and tough Black Hawk defenseman Ed Van Impe, the sticks come up before the gloves come off.

▶
In this remarkable low-angle shot, the total concentration of the players is evident through their similar facial expressions. From left to right, Ron Ellis, Red Kelly, Tim Horton, Johnny Bucyk and Pit Martin battle for possession on a snow-covered ice surface.

▼

Eddie Shack proved he could be more than just an entertainer on the ice by recording 20-goal seasons with five of the six NHL teams he played for during his 17-year career. On January 21, 1967, the Leafs met the Detroit Red Wings at Maple Leaf Gardens. Eight seconds after Bruce MacGregor scored to give the Wings a 5–3 lead, Shack broke away from Gordie Howe and flipped this backhand behind Roger Crozier. The Wings held on for a 5–4 victory, sending the Leafs on a 10-game losing streak that put Punch Imlach in hospital and nearly put the Leafs out of the playoffs.

▶

Frank Prazak was one of the first hockey photographers to position his camera directly over the net. He placed a camera in the rafters, focused it on the net below, and operated it by remote control. The results were dramatic images such as this one, where once again the entire ice surface seems to belong to Jean Beliveau (4) and Johnny Bower. The faint vertical streaks on the ice surface to the right of the net indicate the location of refrigeration pipes from the Montreal Forum's ice-making plant.

The struggle to maintain possession of the puck is the center-piece of this action shot from the 1964–65 campaign. At 6'1" and 205 lbs., Chicago's Phil Esposito (7) was one of the larger players in the game, but he was more than matched by 6'2" Montreal defenseman Jacques Laperriere. Although he weighed only 190 pounds, Laperriere's lanky frame and long reach enabled him to become one of the League's best rearguards.

Eddie Johnston comes out past the top of his crease to cut down the angle as Bruin defenseman Don Awrey (26) attempts to ride Frank Mahovlich off the puck. Johnston was the last NHL goaltender to play every minute of every game in a single season, appearing in all 70 games for the Boston Bruins during the 1963–64 season.

After 13 seasons with the Maple Leafs, Ron Stewart was traded to the Boston Bruins in June 1965. In this January 29, 1966, game against his former mates, Stewart (12) gains a small measure of revenge by blasting this wrist shot under the glove of Terry Sawchuk. Other combatants on the ice include, from left to right, Bob Pulford, Eddie Shack, Larry Hillman, Marcel Pronovost and Pit Martin, whose pretty pass into the slot set up the goal.

By focusing tightly on the action, Prazak manages to capture the ultimate confrontation between goaltender and attacker. Montreal's Henri Richard (16) outraces Jean Ratelle (19) and prepares to pull the puck around the outstretched poke check of New York Ranger netminder Eddie Giacomin in this action from 1965–66.

All three members of the Boston Bruins third line are featured in this photo from a Rangers-Bruins match at Madison Square Garden during the 1966–67 season. The trio of Wayne Connelly (17), Ron Schock (23) and Ron Murphy (28) maneuver behind the Rangers' defense of Harry Howell (3) and Arnie Brown (4) only to have this shot slip just wide of Giacomin in the New York net.

▼

Prazak's camera catches a perfect example of the defensive system the Toronto Maple Leafs used to upset the Chicago Black Hawks in the 1967 semi-finals. In this "three-point" defense, center Red Kelly (4) sets up between the faceoff circles to ward off a third Chicago attacker, Larry Hillman (2) neutralizes Bobby Hull while Marcel Pronovost covers Bill Hay (8), who is about to pounce on this loose puck. When any of these components broke down, Terry Sawchuk was there to thwart the Hawks.

▶

Scenes such as this are commonplace during the Stanley Cup playoffs as players leap off the bench to celebrate a sudden-death victory. The hero in this case was Bob Pulford, whose number 20 jersey can be seen between Allan Stanley (26) and Mike Walton (16). Seconds earlier, Pulford tipped a cross-ice pass from Pete Stemkowski behind Montreal's Rogie Vachon to provide the Maple Leafs with a 3–2 double-overtime victory in game three of the 1967 Stanley Cup Finals. Note the bunting, provincial crests and banner marking Canada's centennial year.

PENALTY
PERIOD
2
OVERTIME
TORONTO
MONTREAL
SCORE
3
TIME TO PLAY
11:34
SCORE
2
NADA
1867 1967
ALL STAR WRESTLING
SUNDAY — 7:30 PM.

▼
Third-year defenseman Bobby Orr (4) arrives on the scene in time to distract Maple Leaf forward Paul Henderson, whose deflection is chested away by Gerry Cheevers during this Boston–Toronto match-up on November 13, 1968. Notice that Cheevers has just started his ritual of painting stitches on his mask, a routine that would become almost as famous as the goaltender himself.

▶
Pittsburgh's Les Binkley snags a shot off the stick of Dave Keon during the unmasked goalie's rookie NHL season in 1967–68. When he was unable to find work as a pro goalie in the early 1960s, Binkley followed the path taken by many other young netminders and signed on to be a trainer/practice goaltender with the AHL's Cleveland Barons. On March 15, 1961, Binkley was called on to replace incumbent Gil Mayer against the first-place Springfield Indians and backstopped the Barons to a 3–2 victory. Binkley captured the Barons' goaltending job with that performance, and went on to play in the AHL, NHL and WHA until 1976.

▼

Detroit's Norm Ullman (7) and Toronto's Marcel Pronovost (3) and Frank Mahovlich (27) watch as Bruce MacGregor (12) outraces Leaf defenseman Duane Rupp in a wrap-around attempt on Johnny Bower during this Red Wing–Maple Leafs clash on October 18, 1967. Ullman had scored at least 20 goals in 11 straight seasons when he was dealt to Toronto in a seven-player deal orchestrated to reverse the hockey fortunes of both teams. Instead, Detroit failed to make the playoffs in 14 of the next 16 seasons while the Maple Leafs didn't win a playoff series until 1974–75, Ullman's last season with the club.

▶

After a disappointing 1969–70 campaign, Ullman (9) rebounded to collect 34 goals and a career-high 85 points in 1970–71. In this early season match-up against the St. Louis Blues, Ullman deposits this pass from Paul Henderson (19) behind Blues' goaltender Ernie Wakely as defenders Terry Crisp (12) and Bob Wall (2) look on in dismay.

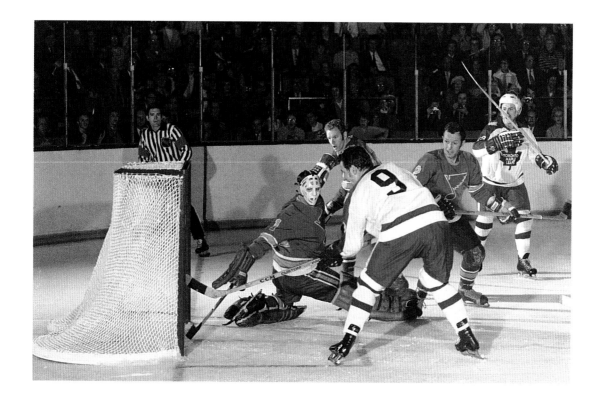

▶

The only player in the history of the NHL to die as a result of an on-ice injury, Bill Masterton wasn't even supposed to be playing professional hockey on January 13, 1968. When the top-rated prospect in the Canadiens' farm system couldn't crack the talented Montreal roster in 1963, Masterton retired to complete his master's degree. Prior to the 1967–68 season, Minnesota North Stars' general manager Wren Blair convinced the Minnesota native to give the NHL one last try, and Masterton agreed. He scored the first goal in franchise history and was enjoying a respectable rookie season when he fell awkwardly to the ice after being checked by California Seals defensemen Larry Cahan and Ron Harris. Masterton struck his head on the ice and was immediately taken to hospital where he died 31 hours later.

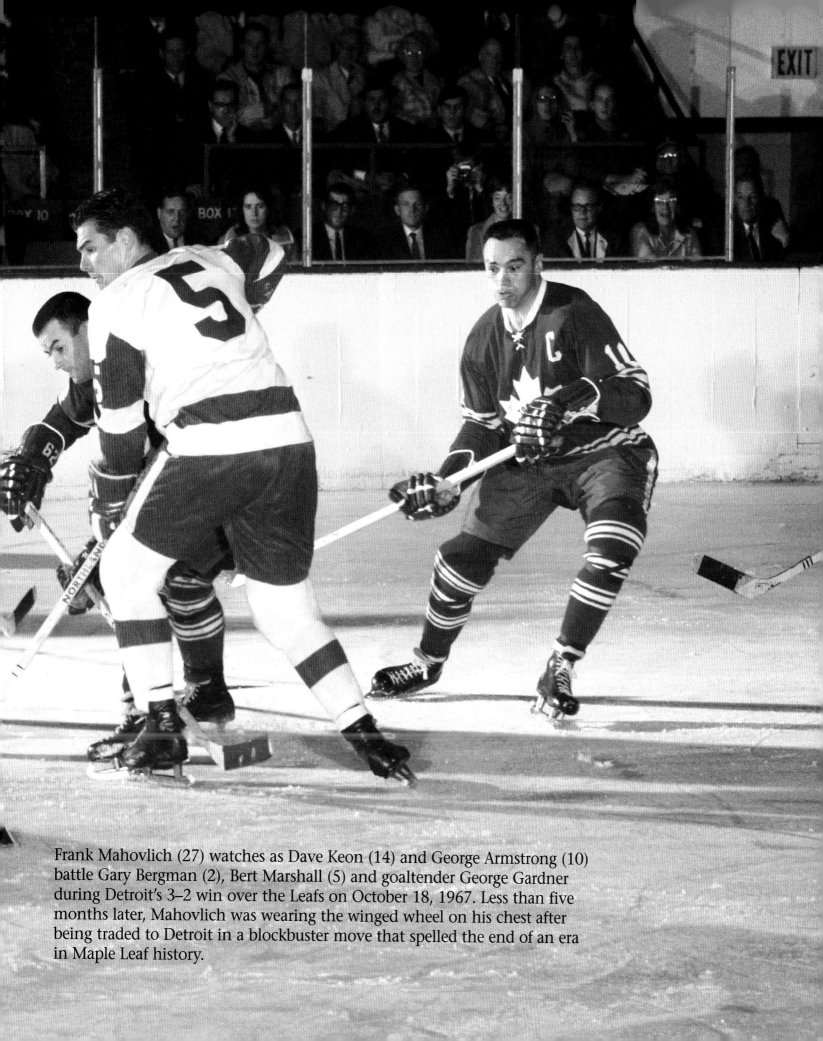

Frank Mahovlich (27) watches as Dave Keon (14) and George Armstrong (10) battle Gary Bergman (2), Bert Marshall (5) and goaltender George Gardner during Detroit's 3–2 win over the Leafs on October 18, 1967. Less than five months later, Mahovlich was wearing the winged wheel on his chest after being traded to Detroit in a blockbuster move that spelled the end of an era in Maple Leaf history.

◄
Montreal defenseman J.C. Tremblay wards off the persistent checking of Maple Leaf captain George Armstrong during this all-Canadian battle on December 11, 1968. Armstrong had a goal and Tremblay had a pair of assists as the Leafs and Habs fought to a 4–4 draw. Note that the photographer's strobe light mounted on the glass above Tremblay is lit in this photo.

▲
When the Detroit Red Wings met Toronto on December 21, 1968, at the Gardens, it marked only the third time that Leaf fans had the opportunity to see Frank Mahovlich wearing a Detroit uniform. Although the "Big M" did manage to score a goal on that evening, for the most part Maple Leaf defenders Pierre Pilote (3), Mike Pelyk (4) and Bruce Gamble (30) kept him in check as the Leafs downed the Wings 8–3.

◀

"Hail" Cesare Maniago was one of the most colorful goaltenders of the early expansion years, combining acrobatics with wild wanderings out of the net. Maniago suited up for the Leafs, Canadiens and Rangers before joining the Minnesota North Stars in 1967–68.

◀▼

Dave Keon, on his way to a 32-goal, 30-assist season, pulls the puck past the outstretched pad of Los Angeles goaltender Gerry Desjardins and slips it in to help the Leafs earn a 4–4 tie with the Kings on November 19, 1969. Desjardins is wearing a mask similar to the one made famous by Terry Sawchuk.

▼

Maple Leaf forward Gary Monahan sends both the puck and a shower of ice over the shoulder of Buffalo Sabre goaltender Roger Crozier. The Sabres joined the NHL in the 1970–71 season with former Leaf general manager Punch Imlach at the controls. Buffalo's uniforms, blue with triple stripes on arm, waist and leg, were based on the old Toronto Maple Leafs design. Imlach suggested the Sabres add gold to their color scheme to show that "We've got more class than Toronto."

In early March 1968, the roof of the Philadelphia Spectrum was destroyed by a severe wind storm, forcing the team to play the remainder of its home games on the road. The Flyers played one game in New York, one game in Toronto and the remainder in Quebec City, home of their farm team. The game played in Toronto on March 8, 1968, against the Boston Bruins was marred by a stick-swinging duel between Larry Zeidel and Eddie Shack midway through the first period. Late in the game, a 2–1 victory for the Bruins, Boston rearguard Gary Doak (25) chased down Philadelphia forward Gary Dornhoefer (12) as Gerry Cheevers looks on.

Boston's Johnny "Pie" McKenzie seems almost airborne as he prepares to shoot against the Leafs on January 14, 1969. Despite his rather odd aerodynamics, McKenzie was able to rip this shot past Toronto goaltender Bruce Gamble, but the Leafs were able to fight back to preserve a 5–5 tie.

▼
While hockey has always been likened to a religion in Quebec, even Canadiens fans sometimes miss worshipping at the Forum, especially if the opposition is a first-year expansion team. An assortment of empty seats greet Atlanta Flames center Curt Bennett as he challenges Ken Dryden during the Flames initial season in the NHL in 1972–73.

▶
Terry O'Reilly (24) and Don Awrey (26) greet Phil Esposito after the crafty Boston center added another goal to his impressive 1972–73 totals. This celebration was repeated 55 times during the season, as Esposito led the NHL in goals for the fourth consecutive campaign.

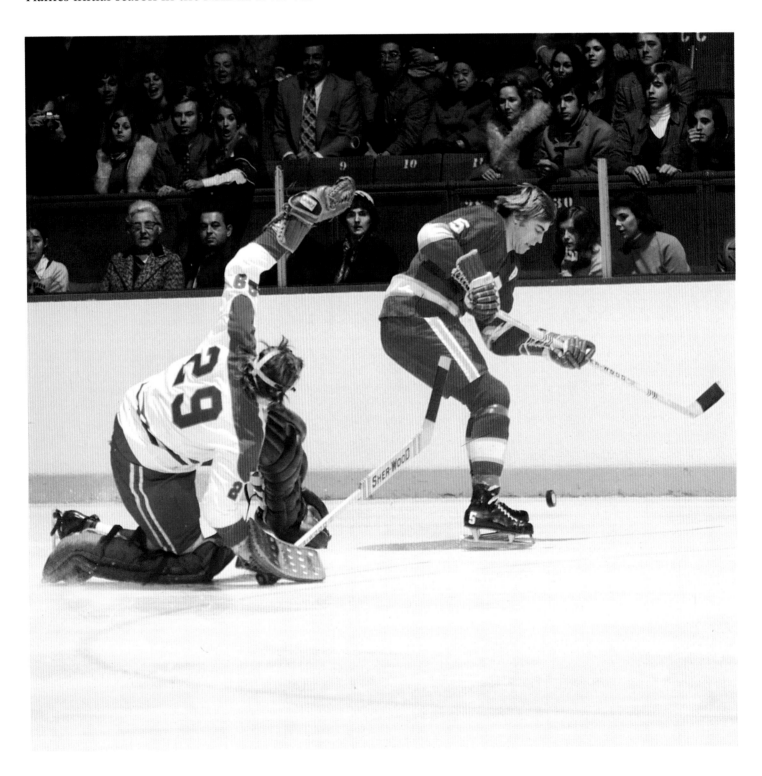

◄
Tony Esposito kicks away this shot during the 1973 Stanley Cup Finals between the Black Hawks and the Montreal Canadiens. Although Esposito had seen 13 games of NHL action with Montreal during the 1968–69 season, he was still considered a rookie when he took over crease duties with the Black Hawks in 1969–70. Esposito quickly earned the nickname Tony "O" by registering 15 shutouts, a freshman record that may never be eclipsed.

▼
Frank Prazak concentrated his lens on the area behind the net more often than most photographers, because the action that took place there largely consisted of one-on-one battles. Here, he captures the determination of Bobby Clarke, as the Philadelphia Flyers captain runs some not-so-subtle interference on Montreal defenseman Guy Lapointe.

This odd but highly effective angle enables the camera to register all the action around the crease. Here, the Buffalo Sabres score on Ken Dryden during the Canadiens' 7–3 victory over the Sabres in the second game of their opening-round playoff series in 1973. Distracting Dryden is Buffalo's Jim Lorentz (8).

▶

Bob Goodenow played four seasons at Harvard, serving as co-captain of the Crimson in 1973–74. He also played on the 1974 and 1975 U.S. National Team. He attended the Washington Capitals first training camp and was assigned to Dayton of the International Hockey League. Some observers believed Bob had the talent to play pro hockey, but Goodenow himself admitted, "I wasn't good enough for the NHL and I wanted to go to law school." After his graduation in 1979, he practiced law for ten years, spending part of his time representing hockey players. He was appointed executive director of the NHL Players' Association on January 21, 1990.

▼

Frank Mahovlich cruises through the crease past the sprawled form of Boston Bruins goalkeeper Gilles Gilbert and the backchecking of Fred Stanfield. Mahovlich's career was regenerated when he was traded to the Canadiens midway through 1970–71. The Big M collected 58 playoff points for Montreal in his four seasons with the team, only two fewer points than he had compiled in 10 playoff appearances with Toronto and Detroit.

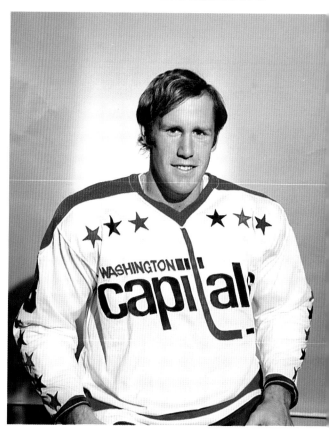

▼

The heart and soul of the Toronto Maple Leafs franchise in the 1970s was Darryl Sittler (27) who became the first Leaf player to register 100 points in a season. Although the Leafs dropped a 7–5 decision in this game against the Los Angeles Kings on January 11, 1975, Sittler eluded enough of the Kings defenders to collect four points.

▶

The Flyers and the Maple Leafs engaged in some spirited battles in the playoffs during the 1970s, but their regular-season match-ups were also rousing affairs. In this March 15, 1975, tilt, Bobby Clarke (16), Borje Salming (21) and Gord McRae (1) fought to a 4–4 draw. In 1974–75, Salming became the first European-trained player named to the NHL All-Star Team.

◄
Jacques Plante played his 21st professional season with the WHA's Edmonton Oilers in 1974–75, compiling a more-than-respectable 3.32 goals-against average in 31 games. Plante, who signed a 10-year contract as the coach, general manager and vice-president of the Quebec Nordiques in 1973, resigned after only one year behind the bench when the Nordiques failed to make the playoffs and posted a $500,000 loss. Moments after stepping down, Plante was signed by the Oilers and spent one final season sweeping the crease in Edmonton.

▼◄
Mike Gartner, the only player in NHL history to score at least 30 goals in 15 consecutive seasons, began his professional career as an under-age junior with the WHA's Cincinnati Stingers in 1978–79. Gartner, who scored 41 goals for Niagara Falls in his final year of junior, managed 27 goals for the Stingers, the fourth-highest total on the team.

▼
Rick Vaive was a 19-year-old rookie when he joined the WHA's Birmingham "Baby" Bulls in 1978 after a 76-goal, 79-assist season with Sherbrooke of the Quebec Junior league in 1977–78. Although he was still a kid outside the rink, Vaive proved himself to be a man on the ice, leading the team with 59 points and leading the league with 248 penalty minutes.

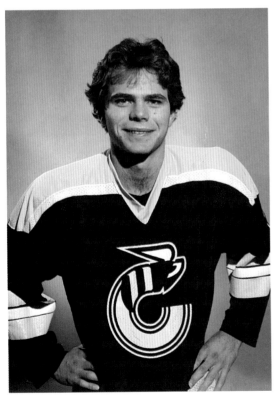

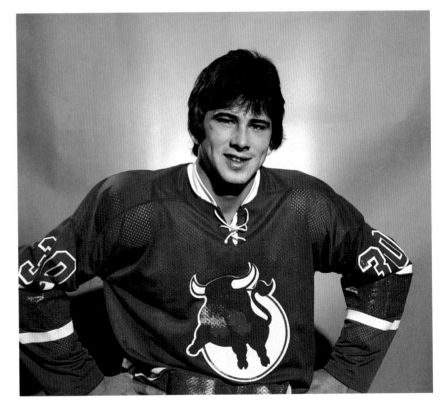

A youthful Mark Messier poses for the camera shortly after making his NHL debut with the Edmonton Oilers in 1979–80. Messier began his professional career as a 17-year-old with the World Hockey Association's Indianapolis Racers, but his rights were assigned to the Cincinnati Stingers when the Racers franchise folded 25 games into the 1978–79 schedule. Messier, who joined fellow under-age junior Mike Gartner in Cincinnati, scored only one goal in 47 games but proved himself to be a feisty competitor with 58 penalty minutes. Note that Messier is wearing skates with molded plastic blade carriers. The old tube skate is finally *passé*.

◄
The heir apparent to the Canadiens' throne previously occupied by Maurice Richard and Jean Beliveau, Guy Lafleur epitomized the "Flying Frenchman" image of the Montreal Canadiens for 14 years. The beauty of Lafleur was the overall efficiency of his game. Never one-dimensional, he recorded six consecutive seasons with at least 50 goals, 50 assists and 100 points from 1974–75 to 1979–80. By 1981–82, when this photo was taken, his hair was thinning and he had lost a step, but his presence on the ice was enough to electrify any fan who longed for those days when winning the Stanley Cup seemed like a pre-ordained right for the Montreal Canadiens.

▶
Brian Bellows, the Minnesota/Dallas Stars all-time leader with 342 goals, is captured by the lens just days before making his All-Star game debut during the 1983–84 season. One of the Stars' most productive offensive leaders, Bellows finished first or second in team scoring in six of his 10 seasons with the club.

▼
Dubbed the "Russian Rocket" because of his outstanding speed and explosive shot, Vancouver's Pavel Bure established himself as one of the NHL's marquee players during the 1993–94 season. After leading the league with 60 goals during the regular season, Bure also topped all goal-scorers during the playoffs, slipping 16 pucks past opposition goalies.

▶
A determined Tim Hunter gets his "game face" on as he prepares for a match during the 1991–92 season, his 11th and final campaign with the Calgary Flames. Throughout his career, Hunter played the game all-out, inspiring his teammates and intimidating his opponents.

▶▼
Keith Tkachuk became one of the youngest captains in NHL history when the Winnipeg Jets awarded him the "C" on November 6, 1993. An accomplished team leader both on the ice and in the dressing room, Tkachuk reached the 20-goal plateau for the third consecutive season in 1994–95.

▶
Los Angeles Kings rearguard Marty McSorley displays the battle scars often associated with the Stanley Cup playoffs. When that big trophy is on the line, the hits get harder, each shift becomes more intense and the pressure keeps building. But as McSorley and every other playoff participant will tell you, summer definitely comes each year, but a chance to win the Stanley Cup may never come again.

◀

Despite being sidelined by injury or illness in seven of his ten NHL seasons, Mario Lemieux has collected 1,211 career points in only 599 games. One of only three players to compile 100 assists in a single season, Lemieux sat out the entire 1994–95 season to recuperate from nagging back injuries and Hodgkin's disease.

▲

Sergei Fedorov joined Ebbie Goodfellow, Sid Abel and Gordie Howe as the only members of the Detroit Red Wings to win the Hart Trophy when he received the prestigious award in 1993–94. Fedorov also became the first player in NHL history to win the MVP award and the Selke Trophy as best defensive forward in the same season.

◀

Although he was only the seventh Clarkson player in the history of the school to be drafted by an NHL club, Dave Taylor still felt he had something to prove. The last player selected (210th overall) by the Los Angeles Kings in the 1975 Amateur Draft, Taylor racked up 110 points in only 34 games in his final season with the Clarkson University Knights. He went on to play 17 seasons with the Los Angeles Kings and became the first player drafted lower than 22nd to register 1,000 career points in the NHL.

▶

Exhibition games between Canadian and U.S. college teams are a highlight of any collegiate season. On Novembver 26, 1994, the York University Yeomen met Cornell University's Big Red at Toronto's Varsity Arena. Cornell's Jake Karam (17) and Mike Sancimino (18) are thwarted by York goaltender Joe Dimaline. Mike Kerekes (19) and Shawn Costello (32) look for the rebound.

◀

Steve Rucchin, who compiled 93 goals and 192 points in four seasons with the University of Western Ontario Mustangs, became one of the few Canadian University players to graduate to the top level when he made his NHL debut during the 1994–95 season. Selected second overall by Anaheim in the 1994 Supplemental Draft, Rucchin collected 17 points and had a plus/minus rating of +7 in 43 games for the Mighty Ducks.

▶
Mike Ramsey entered the 1994–95 season as one of only two members of the gold medal-winning 1980 U.S. Olympic Team still active in the NHL. Ramsey, who spent 14 seasons with Buffalo before joining the Pittsburgh Penguins and Detroit Red Wings, played his college hockey at the University of Minnesota. Ramsey's college and Olympic teammate, Neal Broten, spent the 1994–95 season with Dallas and New Jersey. Dave Christian, an alumnus of the University of North Dakota Fighting Sioux who played for five NHL teams in his 15-year career, played with the Minnesota Moose of the International Hockey league in 1994–95.

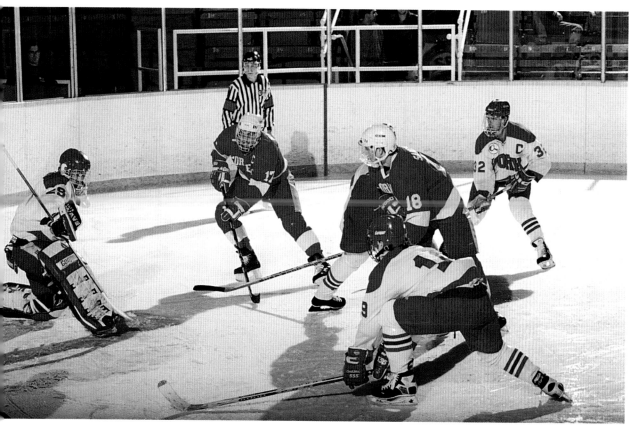

The San Jose Sharks' first selection in the 1994 Entry Draft, Jeff Friesen brought speed and youthful enthusiasm to the Shark-tank during his rookie season. Friesen, who saw action on both the powerplay and penalty-killing units, finished tied for second in team scoring during the 1994–95 season with 15 goals and 25 points.

Patrick Roy guards the Habs net during a 6–4 loss to the Toronto Maple Leafs on February 8, 1992. A rookie sensation during the 1985–86 season with his odd crane-like neck twitches and animated conversations with his goalposts, Roy guided the Canadiens to a surprise Stanley Cup victory in the 1986 playoffs and earned the Conn Smythe Trophy as the post-season's MVP.

One of the most talented young players in the NHL, Ottawa's Alexei Yashin sneaks around the net hoping to catch Hartford goaltender Sean Burke napping. Yashin's ploy worked perfectly, as he tucked the puck just inside the post to give the Senators a 2–1 victory over the Whalers on February 1, 1995.

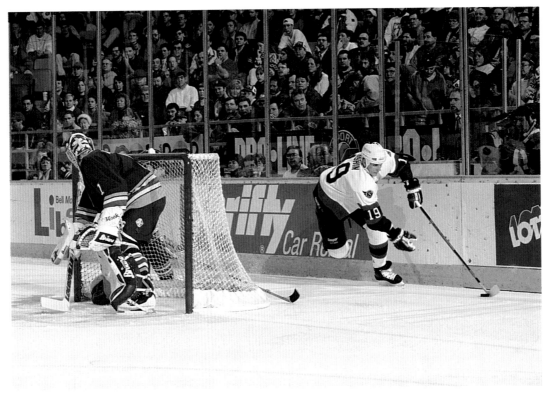

A worried Wayne Gretzky watches as the playoff hopes of the Los Angeles Kings collapse around him late in the 1994–95 season. Despite the Great One's team-leading 48 points and inspired leadership, the Kings' playoff run stalled in the final days of the campaign and the team missed the post-season for the second consecutive year.

Hockey's version of the "Big Hurt," the Philadelphia Flyers' Eric Lindros is the prototype of a team leader in the 1990s: imposing, intelligent, strong and skilled. Despite knee injuries in each of his first two NHL seasons, Lindros topped 40 goals in each campaign. He was named captain of the Flyers for 1994–95 and finished with 29 goals.

HOCKEY HALL OF FAME HONOURED MEMBERS

HONOUR ROLL: There are 300 Honoured Members in the Hockey Hall of Fame. 205 have been inducted as players, 82 as builders and 13 as Referees/Linesmen. In addition, there are 53 media award winners.

(Year of induction to the Hockey Hall of Fame is indicated in brackets after each Member's name.)

PLAYERS

Abel, Sidney Gerald 1969
* Adams, John James "Jack" 1959
Apps, Charles Joseph Sylvanus "Syl" 1961
Armstrong, George Edward 1975
* Bailey, Irvine Wallace "Ace" 1975
* Bain, Donald H. "Dan" 1945
* Baker, Hobart "Hobey" 1945
Barber, William Charles "Bill" 1990
* Barry, Martin J. "Marty" 1965
Bathgate, Andrew James "Andy" 1978
Béliveau, Jean Arthur 1972
* Benedict, Clinton S. 1965
* Bentley, Douglas Wagner 1964
* Bentley, Maxwell H. L. 1966
* Blake, Hector "Toe" 1966
Boivin, Leo Joseph 1986
* Boon, Richard R. "Dickie" 1952
Bossy, Michael 1991
Bouchard, Emile Joseph "Butch" 1966
* Boucher, Frank 1958
* Boucher, George "Buck" 1960
Bower, John William 1976
* Bowie, Russell 1945
Brimsek, Francis Charles 1966
* Broadbent, Harry L. "Punch" 1962
* Broda, Walter Edward "Turk" 1967
Bucyk, John Paul 1981
* Burch, Billy 1974
* Cameron, Harold Hugh "Harry" 1962
Cheevers, Gerald Michael "Gerry" 1985
* Clancy, Francis Michael "King" 1958
* Clapper, Aubrey "Dit" 1947
Clarke, Robert "Bobby" 1987
* Cleghorn, Sprague 1958
* Colville, Neil MacNeil 1967
* Conacher, Charles W. 1961
* Conacher, Lionel Pretoria 1994
* Connell, Alex 1958
* Cook, William Osser 1952
Coulter, Arthur Edmund 1974
Cournoyer, Yvan Serge 1982
* Cowley, William Mailes 1968
* Crawford, Samuel Russell "Rusty" 1962
* Darragh, John Proctor "Jack" 1962
* Davidson, Allan M. "Scotty" 1950
* Day, Clarence Henry "Hap" 1961
Delvecchio, Alex 1977
* Denneny, Cyril "Cy" 1959
Dionne, Marcel 1992
* Drillon, Gordon Arthur 1975
* Drinkwater, Charles Graham 1950
Dryden, Kenneth Wayne 1983
Dumart, Woodrow "Woody" 1992
* Dunderdale, Thomas 1974
* Durnan, William Ronald 1964
* Dutton, Mervyn A. "Red" 1958

* Dye, Cecil Henry "Babe" 1970
Esposito, Anthony James "Tony" 1988
Esposito, Philip Anthony 1984
* Farrell, Arthur F. 1965
Flaman, Ferdinand Charles "Fern" 1990
* Foyston, Frank 1958
* Frederickson, Frank 1958
Gadsby, William Alexander 1970
Gainey, Bob 1992
* Gardiner, Charles Robert "Chuck" 1945
* Gardiner, Herbert Martin "Herb" 1958
* Gardner, James Henry "Jimmy" 1962
Geoffrion, Jos. A. Bernard "Boom Boom" 1972
* Gerard, Eddie 1945
Giacomin, Edward "Eddie" 1987
Gilbert, Rodrigue Gabriel "Rod" 1982
* Gilmour, Hamilton Livingstone "Billy" 1962
* Goheen, Frank Xavier "Moose" 1952
* Goodfellow, Ebenezer R. "Ebbie" 1963
* Grant, Michael "Mike" 1950
* Green, Wilfred "Shorty" 1962
* Griffis, Silas Seth "Si" 1950
* Hainsworth, George 1961
Hall, Glenn Henry 1975
* Hall, Joseph Henry 1961
Harvey, Douglas Norman 1973
* Hay, George 1958
* Hern, William Milton "Riley" 1962
* Hextall, Bryan Aldwyn 1969
* Holmes, Harry "Hap" 1972
* Hooper, Charles Thomas "Tom" 1962
Horner, George Reginald "Red" 1965
* Horton, Miles Gilbert "Tim" 1977
Howe, Gordon 1972
* Howe, Sydney Harris 1965
* Howell, Henry Vernon "Harry" 1979
Hull, Robert Marvin 1983
* Hutton, John Bower "Bouse" 1962
* Hyland, Harry M. 1962
* Irvin, James Dickenson "Dick" 1958
* Jackson, Harvey "Busher" 1971
* Johnson, Ernest "Moose" 1952
* Johnson, Ivan "Ching" 1958
Johnson, Thomas Christian 1970
* Joliat, Aurel 1947
* Keats, Gordon "Duke" 1958
Kelly, Leonard Patrick "Red" 1969
Kennedy, Theodore Samuel "Teeder" 1966
Keon, David Michael 1986
Lach, Elmer James 1966
Lafleur, Guy Damien 1988
* Lalonde, Edouard Charles "Newsy" 1950
Laperriere, Jacques 1987
Lapointe, Guy 1993
Laprade, Edgar 1993
* Laviolette, Jean Baptiste "Jack" 1962
* Lehman, Hugh 1958
Lemaire, Jacques Gerard 1984
* LeSueur, Percy 1961
* Lewis, Herbert A. 1989
Lindsay, Robert Blake Theodore "Ted" 1966
Lumley, Harry 1980
* MacKay, Duncan "Mickey" 1952
Mahovlich, Frank William 1981
* Malone, Joseph "Joe" 1950
* Mantha, Sylvio 1960
* Marshall, John "Jack" 1965

* Maxwell, Fred G. "Steamer" 1962
McDonald, Lanny 1992
* McGee, Frank 1945
* McGimsie, William George "Billy" 1962
* McNamara, George 1958
Mikita, Stanley 1983
Moore, Richard Winston 1974
* Moran, Patrick Joseph "Paddy" 1958
* Morenz, Howie 1945
* Mosienko, William "Billy" 1965
* Nighbor, Frank 1947
* Noble, Edward Reginald "Reg" 1962
* O'Connor, Herbert William "Buddy" 1988
* Oliver, Harry 1967
Olmstead, Murray Bert "Bert" 1985
Orr, Robert Gordon 1979
Parent, Bernard Marcel 1984
Park, Douglas Bradford "Brad" 1988
* Patrick, Joseph Lynn 1980
* Patrick, Lester 1947
Perreault, Gilbert 1990
* Phillips, Tommy 1945
Pilote, Joseph Albert Pierre Paul 1975
* Pitre, Didier "Pit" 1962
* Plante, Joseph Jacques Omer 1978
Potvin, Denis 1991
* Pratt, Walter "Babe" 1966
* Primeau, A. Joseph 1963
Pronovost, Joseph René Marcel 1978
Pulford, Bob 1991
* Pulford, Harvey 1945
Quackenbush, Hubert George "Bill" 1976
* Rankin, Frank 1961
Ratelle, Joseph Gilbert Yvan Jean "Jean" 1985
Rayner, Claude Earl "Chuck" 1973
Reardon, Kenneth Joseph 1966
Richard, Joseph Henri 1979
Richard, Joseph Henri Maurice "Rocket" 1961
* Richardson, George Taylor 1950
* Roberts, Gordon 1971
* Ross, Arthur Howie 1945
* Russel, Blair 1965
* Russell, Ernest 1965
* Ruttan, J.D. "Jack" 1962
Savard, Serge A. 1986
* Sawchuk, Terrance Gordon "Terry" 1971
* Scanlan, Fred 1965
Schmidt, Milton Conrad "Milt" 1961
* Schriner, David "Sweeney" 1962
* Seibert, Earl Walter 1963
* Seibert, Oliver Levi 1961
* Shore, Edward W. "Eddie" 1947
Shutt, Stephen 1993
* Siebert, Albert C. "Babe" 1964
* Simpson, Harold Edward "Bullet Joe" 1962
Sittler, Darryl Glen 1989
* Smith, Alfred E. 1962
Smith, Clint 1991
* Smith, Reginald "Hooley" 1972
* Smith, Thomas James 1973
Smith, William John "Billy" 1993
Stanley, Allan Herbert 1981
* Stanley, Russell "Barney" 1962
* Stewart, John Sherratt "Black Jack" 1964
* Stewart, Nelson "Nels" 1962
* Stuart, Bruce 1961
* Stuart, Hod 1945

* Taylor, Frederic "Cyclone" (O.B.E.) 1947
* Thompson, Cecil R. "Tiny" 1959
  Tretiak, Vladislav 1989
* Trihey, Col. Harry J. 1950
  Ullman, Norman V. Alexander "Norm" 1982
* Vezina, Georges 1945
* Walker, John Phillip "Jack" 1960
* Walsh, Martin "Marty" 1962
* Watson, Harry E. 1962
* Watson, Harry 1994
* Weiland, Ralph "Cooney" 1971
* Westwick, Harry 1962
* Whitcroft, Fred 1962
* Wilson, Gordon Allan "Phat" 1962
  Worsley, Lorne John "Gump" 1980
* Worters, Roy 1969

BUILDERS

* Adams, Weston W. 1972
* Aheam, Thomas Franklin "Frank" 1962
* Ahearne, John Francis "Bunny" 1977
* Allan, Sir Montagu (C.V.O.) 1945
  Allen, Keith 1992
* Ballard, Harold Edwin 1977
* Bauer, Father David 1989
* Bickell, John Paris 1978
  Bowman, Scott 1991
* Brown, George V. 1961
* Brown, Walter A. 1962
* Buckland, Frank 1975
  Bush, Walter 1994
  Butterfield, Jack Arlington 1980
* Calder, Frank 1947
* Campbell, Angus D. 1964
* Campbell, Clarence Sutherland 1966
* Cattarinich, Joseph 1977
* Dandurand, Joseph Viateur "Leo" 1963
  Dilio, Francis Paul 1964
* Dudley, George S. 1958

* Dunn, James A. 1968
  Eagleson, Robert Alan 1989
  Francis, Emile 1982
* Gibson, Dr. John L. "Jack" 1976
* Gorman, Thomas Patrick "Tommy" 1963
* Griffiths, Frank A. 1993
* Hanley, William 1986
* Hay, Charles 1974
* Hendy, James C. 1968
* Hewitt, Foster 1965
* Hewitt, William Abraham 1947
* Hume, Fred J. 1962
* Imlach, George "Punch" 1984
  Ivan, Thomas N. 1974
* Jennings, William M. 1975
* Johnson, Bob 1992
* Juckes, Gordon W. 1979
* Kilpatrick, Gen. John Reed 1960
  Knox, Seymour H. III 1993
* Leader, George Alfred 1969
  LeBel, Robert 1970
* Lockhart, Thomas F. 1965
* Loicq, Paul 1961
* Mariucci, John 1985
  Mathers, Frank 1992
* McLaughlin, Major Frederic 1963
* Milford, John "Jake" 1984
  Molson, Hon. Hartland de Montarville 1973
* Nelson, Francis 1947
* Norris, Bruce A. 1969
* Norris, Sr., James 1958
* Norris, James Dougan 1962
* Northey, William M. 1947
* O'Brien, John Ambrose 1962
  O'Neill, Brian 1994
  Page, Fred 1993
* Patrick, Frank 1958
* Pickard, Allan W. 1958
* Pilous, Rudy 1985

  Poile, Norman "Bud" 1990
  Pollock, Samuel Patterson Smyth 1978
* Raymond, Sen. Donat 1958
* Robertson, John Ross 1947
* Robinson, Claude C. 1947
* Ross, Philip D. 1976
* Selke, Frank J. 1960
  Sinden, Harry James 1983
* Smith, Frank D. 1962
* Smythe, Conn 1958
  Snider, Edward M. 1988
* Stanley of Preston, Lord (G.C.B.) 1945
* Sutherland, Cap. James T. 1947
* Tarasov, Anatoli V. 1974
* Turner, Lloyd 1958
* Tutt, William Thayer 1978
* Voss, Carl Potter 1974
* Waghorn, Fred C. 1961
* Wirtz, Arthur Michael 1971
* Wirtz, William W. "Bill" 1976
  Ziegler, John A. Jr. 1987

REFEREES/LINESMEN

  Armstrong, Neil 1991
  Ashley, John George 1981
  Chadwick, William L. 1964
  D'Amico, John 1993
* Elliott, Chaucer 1961
* Hayes, George William 1988
* Hewitson, Robert W. 1963
* Ion, Fred J. "Mickey" 1961
  Pavelich, Matt 1987
* Rodden, Michael J. "Mike" 1962
* Smeaton, J. Cooper 1961
  Storey, Roy Alvin "Red" 1967
  Udvari, Frank Joseph 1973

ELMER FERGUSON MEMORIAL AWARD
*In recognition of distinguished members
of the newspaper profession
whose words have brought honor
to journalism and to hockey.
Selected by the Professional Hockey Writers' Association.*

* Barton, Charlie, Buffalo-Courier Express 1985
* Beauchamp, Jacques, Montreal Matin/
    Journal de Montréal 1984
* Brennan, Bill, Detroit News 1987
* Burchard, Jim, New York World Telegram 1984
* Burnett, Red, Toronto Star 1984
* Carroll, Dink, Montreal Gazette 1984
  Coleman, Jim, Southam Newspapers 1984
* Damata, Ted, Chicago Tribune 1984
  Delano, Hugh, New York Post 1991
  Desjardins, Marcel, Montréal La Presse 1984
  Dulmage, Jack, Windsor Star 1984
  Dunnell, Milt, Toronto Star 1984
* Ferguson, Elmer, Montreal Herald/Star 1984
  Fisher, Red, Montreal Star/Gazette 1985
* Fitzgerald, Tom, Boston Globe 1984
  Frayne, Trent, Toronto Telegram/
    Globe and Mail/Sun 1984
  Gross, George, Toronto Telegram/Sun 1985
  Johnston, Dick, Buffalo News 1986
* Laney, Al, New York Herald-Tribune 1984
  Larochelle, Claude, Le Soleil 1989

  L'Esperance, Zotique, Journal de Montréal/
    le Petit Journal 1985
* Mayer, Charles, le Journal de Montréal/
    la Patrie 1985
  MacLeod, Rex, Toronto Globe and Mail/Star 1987
  Monahan, Leo, Boston Daily Record/
    Record-American/Herald American 1986
  Moriarty, Tim, UPI/Newsday 1986
* Nichols, Joe, New York Times 1984
* O'Brien, Andy, Weekend Magazine 1985
  Orr, Frank, Toronto Star 1989
  Olan, Ben, New York Associated Press 1987
* O'Meara, Basil, Montreal Star 1984
  Proudfoot, Jim, Toronto Star 1988
  Raymond, Bertrand, le Journal de Montréal 1990
  Rosa, Fran, Boston Globe 1987
  Strachan, Al, Globe and Mail/Toronto Sun 1993
* Vipond, Jim, Toronto Globe and Mail 1984
  Walter, Lewis, Detroit Times 1984
  Young, Scott, Toronto Globe and Mail
    /Telegram 1988

FOSTER HEWITT MEMORIAL AWARD
*In recognition of members of the
radio and television industry who made
outstanding contributions to their profession
and the game during their career in hockey broadcasting.
Selected by the NHL Broadcasters' Association.*

  Cusick, Fred, Boston 1984
  Darling, Ted, Buffalo 1994
* Gallivan, Danny, Montreal 1984
* Hewitt, Foster, Toronto 1984
  Irvin, Dick, Montreal 1988
* Kelly, Dan, St. Louis 1989
  Lecavelier, René, Montreal 1984
  Lynch, Budd, Detroit 1985
  Martyn, Bruce, Detroit 1991
  McDonald, Jiggs,
    Los Angeles, Atlanta, NY Islanders 1990
* McKnight, Wes, Toronto 1986
  Pettit, Lloyd, Chicago 1986
  Robson, Jim, Vancouver 1992
  Shaver, Al, Minnesota 1993
* Smith, Doug, Montreal 1985
  Wilson, Bob, Boston 1987

*Deceased

Photo Credits

Index

**HOCKEY HALL OF FAME
FOUNDING SPONSORS**
Special thanks to
Blockbuster Video
Bell Canada
Coca-Cola Canada
Household Finance
Ford of Canada
Imperial Oil
Molson Breweries
London Life
TSN/RDS
The Toronto Sun